Praise for 365+1 ways to succeed with ADHD

"Laurie Dupar has done it again! Full of wit and wisdom in bite-sized pieces; what more could someone with ADHD want? Like a box of the finest assorted chocolates. Brilliant and varied tips from some of the best in the ADHD field. Short enough to be read and appreciated even by those who hate to read. Love it!"

~ **Michele Novotni**, Ph.D., ADHD Expert; Psychologist and ADHD Coach; Former President, ADDA; Author of *What Does Everybody Else Know that I Don't*

"I meet all kinds of people with a creeping sense that their attention is out of whack. Laurie's book is perfect for a daily dose of awareness for the diagnosed ADDer, the self-diagnosed, and those who are ADDish or chronically disorganized. You'll love it for its practicality and humor."

~ **Judith Kolberg**, Author, *Conquering Chronic Disorganization* and *ADD-Friendly Ways to Organize Your Life*, www.squallpress.net

"Read *365+1 ways to succeed with ADHD* and you'll quickly develop an interesting, new ADHD recovery vocabulary. 'Comprehensive' is one new and essential ADHD evaluation and treatment word. ADHD, as you know, is more complex than a simple set of labels, and treatment/recovery requires a careful review of multiple issues, many covered in the deeply comprehensive pages of *365+1 ways to succeed with ADHD.* From my perspective, *365+1 ways to succeed with ADHD* is the singular most comprehensive ADHD recovery book available, and I strongly encourage you to read and listen to the abundant array of national experts who provided their best insights for your next recovery steps."

~ **Dr. Charles Parker**, Psychiatrist and Psychopharmacologist at Core Psych and Author of *New ADHD Medication Rules*

"Laurie Dupar has done it again with this new amazing compilation of wisdom from the top experts and practitioners in the field. Just like her first book, this new one is infused with her positive view. Laurie Dupar's devotion to helping people with ADHD live rewarding and strength-based lives is evident. I have her first book in my waiting room, and I frequently see clients pick it up for a few minutes before their appointments, turn randomly to a new page, and always find something that speaks just to them. This new book delivers equally practical wisdom in bite-size pieces. A reader will always find something to help them at the right time in an extremely ADHD friendly format."

~ **Sari Solden**, Psychotherapist, MS, LMFT, and Author
of *Women with Attention Deficit Disorder* and *Journeys Through ADDulthood*

In Loving Memory of

Victoria Ball, M.ED, MCC, SCAC,

&

Kate Kelly, MSN, SCAC

Dedicated colleagues,

You are missed.

The ADHD Awareness Book Project

365+1 ways to

succeed

with ADHD

A WHOLE NEW YEAR'S WORTH OF VALUABLE
TIPS & STRATEGIES FROM THE WORLD'S BEST
ADHD COACHES & EXPERTS

Edited by Laurie Dupar, PMHMP, RN, PCC

365+1 ways to succeed with ADHD

Publisher: Laurie Dupar
Granite Bay, CA

Cover Design by Jodi Burgess design

Content edits by WriteAssociate.com

Get your complimentary
BONUS Audio CD and
co-author extras at:

http://theadhdawarenessbookproject.com/3651-order-page

Have the audio CD shipped to your doorstep and get access to additional co-author interviews and bonuses such as:

- A sneak peak of Dr. Billi's upcoming book and learn how to Leverage ADHD to your ADDvantage

- Paul O'Conner's report on success strategies for ADHD business owners

- Susan Lasky's, The 7-Step Powerplan to Success™ with ADHD pdf handout, and

- Interviews and more ADHD success strategies with Abigail Wurf, Sarah Wright, Sarah Ferman, Dr. Robert L. Wilford, Elaine Taylor-Klaus and Diane Dempster

Register your Amazon receipt and mailing information and we will ship you your BONUS CD complete with 8 exceptional ADHD experts sharing more great tips and resources, along with several other bonuses that our co-authors have provided especially to go with the book!

*Your Amazon receipt number is 17 digits long and spaced like this: 123-1234567-1234567. Just go to the URL page;

http://theadhdawarenessbookproject.com/3651-order-page

Enter your name, address and your Amazon order number: to get your BONUS CD sent out right away!

More About the" ADHD Awareness Book Project"

The ADHD Awareness Book Project began nearly two years ago and is guided by these goals: Provide valuable strategies and tips to help people living with ADHD better succeed, and increase the awareness of ADHD worldwide.

Too often, in the last nine years I've worked as an ADHD Coach, I've met with parents, students and newly-diagnosed adults struggling alone, not knowing that answers to their challenges were available. Many had never heard the term "ADHD." They had no idea there were alternative ways to succeed by doing things that better fit with their ADHD brain style. Frankly, I was tired. I was tired of knowing that people of all ages, from young children to adults in their 70's, were struggling alone with ADHD, unaware that there were answers, resources, hope and help out here. I was not alone.

Almost two years ago, believing in the power of community and the dedication of my colleagues, I announced that I would be coordinating a book of tips and strategies for succeeding with ADHD, featuring as many ADHD experts as possible. I invited all of the ADHD professionals I knew and asked them to invite ADHD professionals they knew to participate in this project. Over 80 co-authors from around the world and from a variety of professions and specialties answered the call and submitted their answers to the question: "What is the best tip or strategy you have to help someone with ADHD succeed?" *The ADHD Awareness Book Project: 365 ways to succeed with ADHD* was their responses.

The first edition was such a success, going to #1 in its category on Amazon.com on the day it was launched, that we knew we had to do it again! *365+1 ways to succeed with ADHD: A Whole New Year's Worth of Valuable Tips & Strategies From the World's Best ADHD Coaches & Experts* was born.

In this second edition, each co-author has once again contributed valuable tips and strategies to help people with ADHD succeed. Within these pages there is something for every reader: that one tip, strategy, resource or idea that will be the answer you are most needing in this moment.

How <u>you</u> are part of the ADHD Awareness Book Project!

Whether this book is for you or for someone you care about, a portion of the proceeds from national bookseller sales of *The ADHD Awareness Book Project: 365+1 ways to succeed with ADHD* will be used to support three international ADHD organizations:

- Children and Adults with Attention Deficit/Hyperactivity Disorder (CHADD)
- Attention Deficit Disorder Association (ADDA)
- ADHD Coaches Organization (ACO)

<u>Thank you</u> for helping us increase the awareness of ADHD!

~Laurie Dupar, Editor,
365+1 ways to succeed with ADHD

How to Use this Book

This book is intended to be "ADD friendly." It is formatted to include a large variety of tips that are short, succinct, easy to read and immediately useable. There is a full year's worth, containing 365 tips (plus one for the leap year) in order to give you lots of variety and choice, without the limitations of calendar dates. This unique format was recommended to me by one of my students, Nik, who told me that putting specific dates on a book for people with ADHD might not be helpful because each person may want to read it their own way. Some of you may want to put it by your bedside and read one tip a day...terrific! Some of you may sit down in one sitting and read all the tips...have fun! Still others, in your very wonderful ADHD style, may thumb through the book, starting wherever it catches your attention, reading from the middle to the end...the end to the middle...or read every other page! It is yours to decide. Enjoy in whatever manner your wonderful ADHD brain chooses!

Contact the co-authors

As you read, if you find a particular tip or strategy especially useful, I encourage you to connect with the book's co-authors via the contact information they have provided. They are looking forward to hearing from you!

We want to hear from you!

Share what this book has meant to you, let me in on your personal favorite ADHD strategy, or tell me about your success story! I would love to hear from you! Please email your comments to <u>Laurie@CoachingforADHD.com</u>, or write a review on Amazon and help others gain insight into the tips and strategies that work for you.

Contents

Dedication

This book is dedicated to people living with ADHD, wherever you are. Your commitment, perseverance and determination for answers about how to live successfully with ADHD are a constant source of inspiration. YOU are the experts. YOU are the source for what we know "works" and what, even though it might make sense that it would work, doesn't.

It is also dedicated to ADHD professionals who are committed to making a positive difference in the lives of people with ADHD. These experts include: doctors, therapists, nutritional experts, coaches, educators, lawyers, accountants, organizational specialists and many more. Many of you chose to share your expertise by being a co-author in this book. Thank you all. I am proud to be your colleague.

Individually, we make a difference in the lives of people with ADHD. Together, there is the bigger possibility to positively change the world's understanding and awareness of ADHD. This book could not have happened without ALL of you. *Thank you*

Acknowledgements

Putting this book together was a labor of love borne by a passion: to make a positive difference in the lives of people with ADHD. In fact, I can say it was with an "ADD spirit" that this book was written and published. I had an idea, and I was determined to make it a reality without thought to the obstacles, road blocks, naysayers or disbelievers. Foremost in my thoughts were you, the people with ADHD I had met and had yet to meet. Always on my mind, I knew that this is what someone with ADHD would do. You would find a way through the obstacles, keep your eye on the goal despite the impossibility and get up each day determined and hopeful to succeed. You were the inspiration. Thank you.

I also want to thank all of the co-authors of *The ADHD Awareness Book Project: 365+1 ways to succeed with ADHD*. Your individual and collective belief, support and contributions to this book have made it a reality. I am humbled by your generosity. And, of course, I want to thank my family, you know who you are; without your constant belief in me and undying patience, this would not have been possible. I love you all. I also want to thank my assistant, Meghan Gehan, who always has my back; my business manager, Nancy Seeger, who is a master at managing my chaos; Jodi Burgess at Jodi Burgess Design, who created the book cover and Tammi Metzler at TheWriteAssociate.com, whose expertise and craft with words helped us all "sparkle." This wouldn't have been possible without all of you. Thank you!

~Laurie Dupar

Introduction

Thirteen years ago, my youngest son was diagnosed with ADHD. As a mental health professional used to having the answers, I uncharacteristically found myself searching for something that would help me better understand this mental health disorder and help him to better manage his challenges. At the time, resources were scarce. Several years later, I discovered ADHD coaching and saw how much of a difference this approach made in helping both of us minimize our struggles and experience success. Surprising even myself, I have been an ADHD coach for the past ten years, and my son has pursued his dream and is serving in the United States Navy.

I never set out to be an ADHD coach. Having earned my Master's degree as a Psychiatric Mental Health Nurse Practitioner, I was prepared to diagnose and treat the whole array of mental health disorders. I would have never believed that understanding, advocating or focusing on working with people diagnosed with ADHD would have been so life-consuming and rewarding. Instead, I have been amazed with the consistent and never-slowing stream of people challenged with this disorder. As an ADHD coach, I get to work with some of the most amazingly brilliant and creative people every day...and these are just my clients. The experts, professionals and specialists who focus on working with people diagnosed with ADHD are equally as incredible.

ADHD is a 24/7 disorder affecting people's ability to focus, pay attention, plan, prioritize and overcome a whole host of other challenges. For some people with ADHD, it is difficult to do less interesting tasks, like homework, bill paying, organizing or planning. The inability to complete these tasks has created huge disorder and chaos in their lives. Others struggle throughout the day with finding motivation or fighting distractions from an inner sense of restlessness, from the moment they wake up to the hours they are trying to fall asleep. That's the thing about ADHD; it is so different for everyone.

There are some amazing international organizations available for people to better understand ADHD. I encourage you to seek out the resources from such organizations as Children and Adults with Attention Deficit Disorder (CHADD), www.chadd.org; Adults with Attention Deficit Disorder Association (ADDA), www.add.org; and the ADHD Coaches Organization (ACO), www.adhdcoaches.org. In addition, there are many books written by authors who really understand the challenges of ADHD, many of whom have contributed to this book. I encourage you to explore their wisdom. I believe we can never know too much about ADHD.

And last but not least, there are the individual professionals who serve the ADHD community. Coaches, doctors, researchers, therapists, nutritionists, educators, lawyers, etc. Over the years, I have been awed at this community's dedication and commitment to serve each in their own way, using their unique strengths, talents and gifts to improve the lives of people with ADHD.

365+1 ways to succeed with ADHD is our second book, full of brand new ways to succeed. The first book, *365 ways to succeed with ADHD* went to #1 in its category on Amazon.com last year. The ADHD Awareness Book Project has been an opportunity for all of these people and resources to come together in one place and share their "gems" with you. It is written with parents, families, children, teachers, teens, college students and adults of all ages in mind. There is literally something for everyone! Drawing from their wide variety of expertise and experience, these experts have offered you their best strategies and tips to help you succeed with ADHD. I know you will enjoy and find value in all of their contributions.

*"Your time is limited, so don't waste it living someone else's life. Don't be trapped by dogma, which is living with the results of other people's thinking. Don't let the noise of **others'** opinions drown out your own inner voice. And most important, have the courage to follow your heart and intuition. They somehow already know what you truly want to become. Everything else is secondary."*

~ Steve Jobs

Do you have an Entrepreneurial Brain Style©?

I am frequently asked, "What is the best job for someone with ADHD?" People with ADHD can be <u>anything</u> they want and are at their best when they are using their innate entrepreneurial brain style to create the job that best fits them. Not surprisingly, people with ADHD are 300% more likely to be entrepreneurs than people without ADHD. Your creativity, out of the box thinking, ability to come up with extraordinary solutions and knack for recognizing possible money-making opportunities make you natural entrepreneurs. Unfortunately, most business owners with this gifted brain style don't know how to unlock its potential or harness its strength and therefore waste time and energy struggling with organization, planning, time management, prioritization, delegation, etc. A good business coach that appreciates your unique ADHD entrepreneurial brain style can help you maximize your innate strengths and build competencies around less-developed areas. What do you *really* want to do?

~Laurie Dupar, ADHD Coach & Expert

Laurie Dupar, Certified ADHD Coach, works with gifted entrepreneurial brain style entrepreneurs to help them create productive and profitable businesses. www.CoachingforADHD.com ~ Laurie@CoachingforADHD.com

How to Alarm Yourself

If you are having trouble getting up in the morning or other times, you need to use an alarm. Put the clock across the room so you will have to get up to turn it off. This is especially helpful in the morning because you have to get out of bed to turn off the sound. If you can program which sound you use, choose the most annoying or obnoxious continuous sound you can find. This method can also be used to get you out of the house by setting the alarm by your door. You don't turn it off until you are ready to exit. Many of my clients also use their phone alarms to remind themselves when to take their ADHD medication.

~Abigail Wurf, M.Ed., CLC

Abigail Wurf coaches executives, entrepreneurs, couples and other adults affected by ADHD, along with high school and college students. Serving Washington DC and nationally. awurf@verizon.net ~ www.abigailwurf.com ~ (202) 244-2234

Get Some Peace of Mind via Peace of Place

Peaceful surroundings equal less stress, plus more happiness and focus. And you can de-clutter your brain by de-cluttering your digs! Here are 4 key tricks of the visual de-cluttering trade:

1) Haven't used something in 6 months? It's probably useless; trash or donate.

2) Get a clutter-busting buddy and give her AUTHORITY.

3) If alone, work in 20-minute spurts, then rest or switch tasks. Don't burn out!

4) Can't figure out what to do with stuff? Cover it or hide it!

Throw Something Out Today

And tomorrow, and the next day. If it has no legitimate, frequent, or strong sentimental function, throw the dang thing out. It's liberating!

Give Stuff Away Every Week

Donate it and get a receipt for your taxes. You'll be putting useless stuff to work 3X: saving you money, saving you space AND saving you stress.

~Alan Brown

Alan Brown, a struggling exec until diagnosed with ADD, crafted the success strategies in ADD Crusher™ videos: interactive tools helping ADDers live to their potential. www.ADDCrusher.com

I'm scared

You want to share your story, build the business, leave your spouse, buy the house, or leave the job. But you're scared. I am too. No matter where you came from or where you are, we are all looking to make more money, make an impact, serve, and live an extraordinary life. You can live any life you want, and it's okay to be scared. I am.

They key is: You do it afraid.

The truth is: If you are afraid, you have company.

The prescription is: Do it anyway.

Any next big step is scary. As my mentor says, "You change ~ adapt ~ grow!" And when you do, you see results. Success takes action, even when you are afraid. Success means being nervous and investing in yourself. Being afraid and starting anyway. Being scared and taking risks. Success is in doing it afraid.

~Suzanne Evans, CEO

Suzanne Evans is the founder of Suzanne Evans Coaching, LLC, ranked #225 in Inc 500 for 2012. She supports, coaches, and teaches over 30,000 women enrolled in her wealth and business-building programs.

For the Non-ADHD Partner: Ask Specifically for What You Want

We tell parents of ADHD children to communicate specifically, in advance and in behavioral terms what we expect of children, describing what the desired outcome looks like.

And it's a great practice for the spouse or partner of the adult with ADHD as well! If there's something that you really need, or a desired outcome that means a lot to you, ask specifically for what you want. "Honey, we've got an important anniversary coming up this weekend. What I want is for both of us to be home from work on Friday by 5:30. Then I want us to have a 5-10 minute conversation about the events of the day. I want us to do this while maintaining eye contact, with our phones in our pockets. Then I want us to shower and change clothes in time to make it to a 7:30 dinner reservation."

~Dr. Nowell, Ph.D.

Dr. Nowell is a Neuropsychologist offering workshops and clinical services. Contact him at www.DrNowell.com to set up a one-hour ADHD Q & A consultation.

The Work Kit Approach to Efficiency

How often have you gotten derailed because you don't have that thing you need? It's easy to go looking for it, get distracted, and not get back to what you were doing. The solution is to create kits so you have everything you need WHERE you need it.

- Put scissors, pens, sticky notes, tape, etc., everywhere you might need them: desk, kitchen, front hall, garage, etc.

- Put a bucket with frequently-used cleaning supplies in the kitchen and every bathroom.

- Have duplicates of frequently-needed household tools: hammers, screwdrivers, pencils, tape measurers, glue, finishing nails, WD40, etc. Keep the ones you use frequently in your own personal toolbox.

- Use see-through Ziploc bags for all of your on-the-go necessities: electronics, personal items, etc. Either keep one to move from purse to briefcase or make one for each place.

~Sarah D. Wright, M.S., A.C.T.

Nationally-known ADHD coach Sarah D. Wright specializes in helping professionals in small businesses get on track and get going. FocusForEffectiveness.com ~ Sarah@FocusForEffectiveness.com (858) 408-9338.

"ADD" or "ADHD"?

66"Is it called ADD or ADHD?" is a question I get frequently and is understandably confusing, because both are used these days interchangeably! The correct professional term is "ADHD," which stands for Attention Deficit Hyperactivity Disorder. It is an "umbrella" term for all the different subtypes of ADHD. When someone is diagnosed with a particular subtype of ADHD, it is professionally correct to call it "ADHD Combined Type" (both hyperactivity and inattentiveness) or "ADHD Predominantly Inattentive Type" or "ADHD Predominantly Hyperactive-Impulsive Type."

The term "ADD," which stands for Attention Deficit Disorder, is commonly used by many people in the general public and the media. I am not sure why. Perhaps it is simply easier to say; however, it is not the professionally correct term. However you spell it or say it, as "ADD" or "ADHD," is fine.

~Laurie Dupar, PMHNP, RN, PCC, Certified ADHD Coach and Nurse Practitioner

Laurie Dupar, PMHNP, RN, PCC, is a trained psychiatric mental health nurse practitioner and certified ADHD coach. You can find out more at www.coachingforadhd.com.

Containers

Having ADHD requires me to incorporate containers for just about everything. The containers create boundaries, become homes for things or thoughts, define spaces, decrease stress, create personal safety, save time, aid focus, keep things safe, organize time and space, etc. They don't have to be physical and are often invisible; however, for me, they are invaluable. I use many types of containers to make my ADHD brain work better and my life easier.

Here are some examples of my containers: meditation, timers, watches, clocks, to-do lists, calendars, deadlines, bookcases, envelopes, computers, file drawers, trash cans, boxes, body doubles, boundaries, baskets, bulletin boards, post-it notes, floors, and backs of doors.

What types of containers can you incorporate to assist your ADHD and benefit your life?

~Dee Shofner Doochin, MLAS, PCC, CMC, PACG, SCAC

Dee Shofner Doochin, MLAS; Professional Certified Coach; Certified Mentor Coach; Senior Certified ADHD Coach; wife, mother, grandmother, and great-grandmother with ADHD; adventurer; lover of life! www.deedoochin.com

Put a Whiteboard in Front of Your Face

Whatever is not front of mind does not exist for someone with ADHD. Set up whiteboards in high-traffic areas: on the refrigerator, facing your desk at the office, at the door where you leave the house, etc. Use these whiteboards for important information you need at each spot. The refrigerator door is a good place to post the family schedule. The front door is a good place to have a checklist of what you need before you leave the house. In front of your desk is a great place for you to keep a listing of your appointments and task lists. With a whiteboard, you can erase what you no longer need, reprioritize what is already there and/or add new items.

~Alan R. Graham, Ph.D., PCC, SCAC

Alan R. Graham, Ph.D., PCC, SCAC, trains ADD coaches for Mentorcoach, coaches executives with business and organizational challenges, and works with ADHD adults, teens, children and parents. www.ADDvisor.com ~ (847) 824-1235

Don't DO; BE

Your turbo ADHD brain creates the cutting edge of the ever-expanding universes with the thoughts that you think. Hamburger linear processing starts with a chuck roast, and grinds it in a meat grinder (DO) in order to (HAVE) a hamburger (mediocre lunch blahs).

ADHD brains start with being happy, extraordinary, innovative, and wealthy, which calls forth a plan for fulfillment from the future and DOING in order to HAVE the invention, self-esteem, and mastery desired. ADHD brains are the operating system of the Aquarian age.

~Nancy Anne Brighton, LCSW, ADHD Coach

Nancy Anne Brighton, LCSW, ADHD Coach, empowers gifted adults with upside-down brilliance to create compelling futures from the future. Bright Brains Building. Brighter Future. www.BrightONBrains.com ~ ADHDcoach@BrightonBrains.com ~ (386) 290-6703

Visualize for Peace and Calm

Here is another brain-based strategy for when you feel over the top or panicked: Visualize a word or sentence. Choose it ahead of time as an auditory cue to help keep you calm, then do these three simple steps:

1. Picture the word or sentence as a mental image.
2. Color it in, stroke by stroke, like a painter in your brain.
3. Now, see that word or sentence in your head and lay on your belly and put your arms and legs out like superman.

I know you feel silly, but mental imagery combined with motor movement has been transforming athletes into Olympians for over 20 years. The combination of visualizing the word while holding your limbs up activates both thinking and motor neurons at the same time. This action calms your limbic brain and allows your brain to focus on what really counts: your peace of mind.

~Lynne Kenney, Psy.D.

Lynne Kenney, Psy.D., is a mother of two, a practicing pediatric psychologist in Scottsdale, AZ, and the creator of The Family Coach Method. Her NEW co-authored book, *Time-In not Time-Out*, is available this Fall on Kindle. For more visit www.lynnekenney.com.

How to Prioritize When Ideas Pop Out of Your Head Like Flavors at a Chocolate Factory

For ADHD minds, prioritizing tasks and goals can be challenging. Having frequent ideas generates newer goals, leading to greater interest in newer tasks. Older tasks may seem mundane, boring or disconnected from purpose, making it harder to assign them priority. To gain clarity, I suggest beginning by breathing and creating a calm, peaceful state, but this technique can be effective on the go as well. Visualize your tasks as knots on various golden threads, each heading toward different goals. Each knot is another task towards achieving a goal. Follow your golden threads, asking: *What goal does this connect to? Is it my goal? Is it aligned with my core purposes and values? Am I passionate about this? Does it support work I've already completed? Will it contribute to my well-being or the well-being of others?* Threads with more positive answers deserve more priority and time from you.

~ Jonathan Salem, M.S.

Jonathan Salem, M.S. Specializes in Entrepreneurship, Applied Technology, and coaching clients with ADHD and/or Mild to Moderate Traumatic Brain Injury. (409) ADHD-NOW (409) 234-3669 ~ Jon@CoachADHDNow.com

How is ADHD Treated?

"How do I treat my ADHD?" is a common question I get from new clients diagnosed with ADHD. Currently, there are a number of ways to treat ADHD, or minimize the symptoms, and multiple theories about which is the best. Medical treatment is one approach and involves medication to rebalance the neurotransmitters in the brain. Another common approach is focusing on a healthy lifestyle, concentrating on diet, exercise and consistent sleep.

Following studies that suggest that people with ADHD have common deficiencies in omega-3 fatty acids, vitamin C, B6, iron, magnesium and zinc, some people try to manage their challenges through diet and supplements. Some have found success with increased focusing using neurofeedback. Others approach the treatment of ADHD through behavior modification techniques. The most successful approach to reduce or minimize the challenges of ADHD is often based on you as an individual and is a combination of these.

~Laurie Dupar, PMHNP, RN, PCC, Certified ADHD Coach and Nurse Practitioner

Laurie Dupar, PMHNP, RN, PCC, is a trained psychiatric mental health nurse practitioner and certified ADHD coach. You can find out more at www.coachingforadhd.com.

Virtual Assistants

D o you often pay late fees on your bills? Even when you have the money to pay on time? Have you received a ticket for not renewing your car registration on time even though you were sent a reminder and can do it online?

If any of these are true, you need help. You can automate, but some bills and other obligations may not be regular enough or require some scrutiny before being paid. But you can't, don't or won't do it yourself.

That is when a VA can help. A VA is a Virtual Assistant whom you can hire to handle these things so you can stop worrying. Vas work either independently or for a company of Virtual Assistants and are usually paid an hourly rate. Solo practitioners might be a good source to recommend a VA, or you can search online for a good Virtual Assistant.

~Abigail Wurf, M.Ed., CLC

Abigail Wurf, M.Ed., CLC coaches executives, entrepreneurs, couples and other adults affected by ADHD. Washington DC and nationally. awurf@verizon.net ~ www.abigailwurf.com ~ (202) 244-2234

Is it Hot in Here or is it Just Me?

Women at "that certain age" are more likely to be diagnosed with ADHD because estrogen is on a rollercoaster. Estrogen helps those darned neurotransmitters make better connections in the brain. It makes sense to have your hormone levels checked if you are 40-or-better and feeling a little "dain bread" (translation: "brain dead"). If you're a few quarts low on estrogen, your doctor may prescribe low dose birth control pills, or hormone replacement therapy, if your medical history allows. ADHD medications are less effective when estrogen levels are low, so talk to your ADHD doctor about changing your dosage, too. The hot flashes will pass; but the ADHD will stick around.

~Linda Roggli, PCC

Linda Roggli, PCC; award-winning author of *Confessions of an ADDiva - Midlife in the Non-Linear Lane* and ADHD coach/retreat facilitator, supporting women 40-and-better at www.addiva.net.

MPPD?

If you are a procrastinator, or have Multiple Project Personality Disorder, this is for you!

Here are the 10 F's to help you finish any project:

1. Get the **Fundamentals** down. **Finalize** project ideas and **Figure** out what is needed.

2. **Formulate** a plan based on **Facts**, desired outcome and either a deadline or amount of time needed.

3. **Focus** your attention on one step of the plan at a time.

4. **Follow through** on your plan. Keep the **Faith** and keep moving **Forward** if and when things get tough.

5. **FINISH!** Stay with it all the way to the end. Sometimes when the hard parts are over, we think we are done. The devil is in the details of the last 20% of the project.

Celebrate and share your success!

~*Kricket Harrison, CPCC, ACC, PACG,*
Professional Coach & Speaker

Kricket Harrison, Professional Coach & Creator of the SMARTSuccess™ Club, an online accountability program for procrastinators and project-do'ers everywhere! www.SMARTSuccessClub.com

"You are never too old to set another goal or dream another dream."

~ Les Brown

Identify and Thrive on Your High Activity Time

A trap for individuals with an entrepreneurial brain is to act against their inherited patterns of activity levels to fit the conventional mold of Monday-Friday, 9-5 productivity. For individuals on the kinetic end of the activity-level spectrum, like most entrepreneurs, it helps to identify and embrace your inherited high-activity periods. This time is, in a sense, a super-power, with the potential to make you far more productive than most people. To maximize your high-activity time:

1. Observe when you have your high-activity periods (a lot of energy and ability to focus).

2. Schedule your most demanding projects - maybe developing new products or business ideas - to that time.

3. For this strategy to work, your high-activity time must always be followed by a period of rest, in order for your brain to recharge and ensure your well-being over time.

~Anna Maria Lindell

Anna Maria Lindell, ADDCA graduate. Helping entre- and intrapreneurs to increase productivity. Co-founder of the ACO Global Expansion Committee. www.facebook.com/advancesweden.se ~ www.advancesweden.se

Top 7 Ways to Focus at Your Desk

Focusing at your desk is difficult with ADHD, as distractions are plentiful. Next time you need to focus at your desk, try one of these strategies:

- When listening to a conference call, take detailed notes, put your computer into sleep or hibernate mode, and sit with your back to your computer.
- Take time out of your day to exercise. Even a five-minute burst can help you refocus.
- Organize your desk to keep the clutter from overwhelming you.
- Find a drawer where you can store your most distracting items.
- Work on one project at a time. Your effectiveness decreases when you try to multitask.
- Turn off email and your web browser if you do not need them for your current task.
- Put a "Do Not Disturb" sign up to discourage interruptions from others.

~Laura Rolands, ADHD Coach

Laura Rolands is an ADHD Coach who helps clients manage time, focus on priorities, pay attention, increase productivity and achieve goals. Learn more at www.MyAttentionCoach.com.

DON'T Live Up to Your Potential!

So many times, I hear, "I am just not living up to my potential." My clients beat themselves up with those words, feeling worse and worse about who they are and what they do. Forget about potential. That is something we have no control over, and it is a vague concept that really is meaningless. So, the next time you feel bad about where you should be, take a pause. Instead of comparing yourself to where you "should be," compare yourself to where you've come from. You will be amazed at how that sets you up for feeling great. Trust me, you're more likely to reach your potential feeling good then beating yourself into submission.

~Roger DeWitt, PCC, BCC

Roger DeWitt, PCC, BCC, ADHD Coach for Creative Executives and the Entertainment Industry. www.adhdcoachnyc.com

The White Round Carpet Strategy

In my family, we are three women (my daughters, aged 9 and 6, and me). Sometimes we tend to lose our temper... but smashing doors or shouts of "Mom - you scare me" doesn't have to be the norm.

When we get angry with each other, we have a great rule. Everybody takes a few minutes to calm down, then we meet in the hall, sit on our carpet, and each gets the time to share her point of view. Sometimes it's time to apologize and hug each other. This meeting solves most of our conflicts quickly and easily. I rarely need any punishment for my kids because they often feel sorry already.

~Cordula Bredemeier, ADD Coach

Cordula Bredemeier, Educator, ADD Coach (AAC, trained by ADD Coach Academy), coaches in German and English. Learn more about Cordula at www.StayinConnection.com: coaching for stressed parents.

Managing To-Do Tasks

We get optimistic making a to-do list. But we may have a list that could take years to complete! Make two lists, one (your "do now" list) that contains what you can complete within two weeks and one that contains all the rest of the things you want to work on later (your "someday" list). Assign dates for as many as you can.

Take all the tasks in the first list and write them in your planner (paper, electronic, telephone, or computer) at a specific time and date when you expect to be able to do them.

Prioritize your second list of actions (your "Someday Tasks" list) according to their importance. Break these tasks into smaller steps that can be completed in a short time. Move some of these to your "to do" list as you find time in your schedule. Follow your planned activities; watch the work get done!

~ Hervé J. LeBoeuf, III, Ph.D.

Dr. LeBoeuf, Life and ADHD Coach, leads people with ADHD, of all ages and worldwide, to success by working with their unique brains. HLeBoeuf@Gmail.com ~ (703) 455-4144

Are You Jet Lagged?

Every weekend, people with ADHD fly coast to coast. Not literally, of course, but when you stay up late on weekends or sleep in late on days off, your body reacts as if you had flown from San Francisco to New York and back!

Sleeping when you have ADHD is already challenging. Staggering your sleep patterns just makes a difficult situation worse. Every time you change your sleep or waking time more than an hour either way, it takes your body three days to recover. Just imagine…when you stay up late on Saturday or sleep until noon on Sunday, it takes your body until Wednesday to readjust.

Consistent sleep, which includes going to bed and getting up at the same time, is one of the most effective strategies to managing your ADHD symptoms. So keep those sleep times consistent, or you will feel like you jetted around the globe without even enjoying the scenery.

~Laurie Dupar, PMHNP, RN, PCC, Certified ADHD Coach and Nurse Practitioner

Laurie Dupar is a trained psychiatric nurse practitioner, ADHD coach and author. You can reach her at (916) 791 1799 or www.coachingforadhd.com.

Take Back Your Life

As parents, we convince ourselves that everyone else's needs matter more than our own. We'll get to ourselves eventually, right? Wrong! Martyring ourselves for our kids isn't good for anyone – especially our kids!

What's so important about paying attention to yourself?

For you: happy parents → happy kids. When you're feeling more like a whole person, everyone in your family benefits. You know it's true. What if you believe it?

For kids: you are your kids' best curriculum. Want your kids to learn to take care of themselves? Show them how. Model it for them. Exercise. Eat well. Get sleep. Turn off screens. Get a coach for yourself. Get a job. Whatever you know you want that you've been pretending isn't really important to you -- put it back on your list, and move it up to the top!

~ Elaine Taylor-Klaus, CPCC, ACC, and
Diane Dempster, MHSA, CPC, ACC

ImpactADHD helps parents help kids. Elaine Taylor-Klaus & Diane Dempster provide reality-based training, with coaching to make it stick. We help your family thrive! http://www.ImpactADHD.com

The Music of Your Life

Many of my clients with ADHD feel like their life is in a constant state of chaos or crisis. To help them pinpoint the source of that frenzy, I ask them to envision their life as if it's a symphony. I have them assign the various instruments to different realms of their life and take an inventory of the different emotions that come from these areas. For example, the violin's happy melody could represent family life. Perhaps the constant hammering on the piano represents work or social life. Maybe the loud thud and boom of the drums represents fear or procrastination. I ask them to step back and look at how the symphony sounds - is there too much noise coming from one area that's causing chaos? This is a great way to see the various components of your life holistically and figure out what's specifically bringing disharmony to it.

~Dr. Billi

The AttentionB Method, Pedagogical/Class Management for ADHD with Dr. Billi, Ph.D. Tame the chaos in your classroom using my unique strategies. www.AttentionB.com ~ DrBilli@AttentionB.com ~ (855) DrBilli

ADHD Is Not ADHD

ADHD diagnosis and treatment is controversial simply because it's so poorly understood and too often treated without a specific plan or set of medication measurements. "Hyperactive" and "inattentive" don't adequately describe you or your problems. Those diagnoses often don't describe the underlying conflict, and neither diagnosis fits who you are on the inside. It's natural that you feel misunderstood.

If you begin to think more about brain function, you will quickly realize that many who suffer with ADHD symptoms don't suffer with an Attention *Deficit* Disorder. In fact, most suffer from Attention *Abundance* Disorder: too many thoughts. No wonder the diagnosis is so confusing; this finding is not in the diagnostic manual. It's reassuring to know you can be understood in the context of new brain information, and that better medication targets ultimately improve medical outcomes.

~Dr. Charles Parker

Dr Charles Parker, Author, Neuroscience Consultant, Psychiatrist, Psychopharmacologist. About: http://bit.ly/boutcp. Teaching: CoreBrain.org. Treatment Systems: CorePsych.com. *ADHD Medication Rules.* Amazon: http://bit.ly/ruleswork.

Is Your "Filter" Full?

Having ADHD means that the brain is busy most of the time with an assortment of thoughts or ideas. Having ADHD also means that we are less likely to have the full ability to filter our thoughts or stimuli in the environment. If we are not taking the time each day, or even several times each day, to check and see if our 'filter is full', this hyperactivity or overabundance of mental or environmental activity can often lead to feeling overwhelmed and eventually shutting down. It's a bit like the difference between experiencing the world with gentle waves washing up on the beach verses a tsunami that completely washes us out! Making sure we are pausing during our day to clear our thoughts, or down load them into a planner or other reminder system, will help to keep that filter clear so we can move forward.

~Laurie Dupar, PMHNP, RN, PCC, Certified ADHD Coach and Nurse Practitioner

Laurie Dupar is a Certified ADHD Coach and author of the popular book, *Brain Surfing and 31 Other Amazing Qualities of ADHD*. Download your ebook copy now: www.coachingforadhd.com.

Help! I've Fallen Off the Track and I Can't Get Back!

Getting distracted is easy; staying on task sometimes isn't! Here are ten tips to help you get focused and stay focused. Pick and choose which ones work for you, but do not do all at the same time!

1. Before you start, make a step-by-step plan so you don't get overwhelmed.

2. Make sure you've got water and some healthy snacks nearby.

3. Use the system you're comfortable with, even if it's not what the "experts" say works best.

4. Take short breaks - don't wear your brain out!

5. If you're in a rut, get up and move! Walk around, jump in place, change locations, etc.

6. Ask for help or suggestions if you get stuck.

7. Try some deep breathing if you start to feel overwhelmed.

8. Work in short increments; use a timer if that helps.

9. Always stay positive!

10. Reward yourself for a job well done (or partially done)!

~Dr. Laurie Senders, Ph.D.

Laurie Senders, PhD., Certified Life Coach and ADHD Coach who transforms women entrepreneurs into organized, time-oriented, money-producing professionals. drlsenders@comcast.net

Find Time to Keep up with the World (Without Getting Lost on the Web)

A client of mine keeps a clock radio in her bathroom, tuned to an all-news station. It's the kind with a 15-minute sleep button. Whenever she goes into the bathroom - for any reason - she hits that button. Voila! The latest news. She's in no danger of getting trapped in current events hyperfocus; the sleep button turns off the radio after 15 minutes, reminding her to move along. And those times she's hyperfocused on what she needs to do next, she doesn't have to wonder later if she turned the darn thing off when she left the bathroom! Since initiating this system, she has found the willpower to avoid clicking those tantalizing news links. Having increased the likelihood that she will stay focused on why she went to the internet to begin with, she no longer fears paying bills online (solving a few other problems as well).

~Madelyn Griffith-Haynie, CTP, CMC, A.C.T., MCC, SCAC

Madelyn Griffith-Haynie, global ADD expert, multi-certified coaching pioneer, ADD coaching field co-founder, brain-based trainer, neuro-diversity advocate, and speaker, helps clients transform *can't* to *capable*. mgh@addcoach.com ~ www.ADDandSoMuchMore.com

Blurting

If you blurt out things, speak out of turn, interrupt because you are impatient or feel your thought can't wait, you are not alone. Many people with ADHD have this problem. These actions are called blurting and relate to our impulsivity, or our inability to pause before acting.

Socially, you have many options. You can excuse yourself from the group, get something to eat or move to another group. If you are one on one, you can be mindful: take a deep breath and slowly release it while trying to clear your mind. You can try to think of a question to ask. Thinking gives you time to tune in and get up-to-date in the conversation. Once you formulate a question, wait for a pause to raise the question, or if the moment has passed, just let go of it. Your spurt of energy will have been released.

~Abigail Wurf, M.Ed., CLC

Abigail Wurf coaches executives, entrepreneurs, couples and other adults affected by ADHD, as well as high school and college students. Available in Washington DC and nationally. awurf@verizon.net ~ www.abigailwurf.com ~ (202) 244-2234

Choice

Are you aware that all of life is a choice? Yep...life is made up of two kinds of choices -- unconscious choices and conscious choices.

Unconscious choices are when you allow other people, situations or circumstances to make choices for you and then you say, "I had to do that, I didn't have a choice." In reality, you actually made an unconscious choice to allow the choice to be made by someone or something other than you. Conscious choices are those you make for yourself, often after lots of thought or sometimes on the spur of the moment by listening to your intuition, or gut.

~Dee Shofner Doochin, MLAS, PCC, CMC, PACG, SCAC

Dee Shofner Doochin, MLAS; Professional Certified Coach; Certified Mentor Coach; Senior Certified ADHD Coach; wife, mother, grandmother, and great-grandmother with ADHD; adventurer; lover of life! www.deedoochin.com

Make it Fun

A few tips to get you through unpleasant tasks:

1. Sing what you're thinking while you're cleaning.

2. Light candles or incense to initiate doing a chore.

3. Dance while you work (I wrote these tips wearing a glittery blue scarf).

4. Put on lipstick to wash the dishes.

5. Got messy clutter? Play the *Throw Away 5 Pieces of Trash* game.

6. Fake it 'til ya make it - actually pretend like what you're doing is exciting.

7. Set the timer for the 5-minutes game - and attack your activity for 5 minutes.

8. Time yourself with a stopwatch to see how long it takes you to do an activity.

9. Allow yourself 1 minute before doing a chore to really let loose and complain about doing the task (either in writing or aloud to yourself or someone else).

You'll most likely wind up laughing out loud to yourself.

~Aimee Green, MLIS, MSSW, ADHD Coach

Aimee Green MLIS, MSSW, ADHD Coach & Organizer for Adults & College Students. Austin, Texas. www.austinADDcoaching.com ~ aimee@aimeegreen.net ~ (512) 230-5477

Reduce Stress and Fall Asleep Faster with a Simple Brain Exercise

Do you find yourself lying awake even when you're tired? Does your brain keep going and won't let you sleep?

Here's a simple technique to calm a part of your brain that's keeping you awake. Close your eyes. Have a friend hold their hands a few inches to either side of your head. They surprise you with a light finger click in one ear or the other, and you turn your head in the *opposite* direction and then back to center. This head-turn exercise puts a check on your stay alert, turn-and-look reaction, and it helps calm the part of your brain that is keeping you awake at night. You can watch a video demonstration of this and other stress-reducing exercises at www.BrainTimeVideos.com.

~ Dr. Jim Otis, Fellow, American College of Functional Neurology

Dr. Otis specializes in drug-free treatment for ADHD and Learning Disabilities and is the inventor of BrainTime™, a patent-pending technology for optimal brain health. www.BrainTimeVideos.com

Stop the Rebound

"Rebound" is the tendency of some medications, as they wear off, to cause a return of the symptoms they relieved. Rebound is common with caffeine, over-the-counter pain medications, alcohol, decongestants and ADHD medications. Rebound symptoms might include restlessness, moodiness, headache, irritability, tiredness or increase in appetite. As always, talk with your doctor about your concerns. Experiencing rebound is not always a reason to stop taking your medication. Sometimes rebound can be minimized by taking a small dose of medication right before the first wears off or doing things that naturally increase the dopamine levels in your brain, such as doing physical activities around that time of the day; drinking a small cup of coffee, tea, caffeinated soda, or chocolate milk; or eating a small square of dark chocolate. Chocolate, caffeine and exercise release small amounts of dopamine in your brain that should reduce the rebound and keep you in the game!

~Laurie Dupar, PMHNP, RN, PCC, Certified ADHD Coach and Nurse Practitioner

Laurie Dupar is a Certified ADHD Coach and author of the popular book, *Brain Surfing and 31 Other Amazing Qualities of ADHD*. Download your ebook copy now at www.coachingforadhd.com.

Discover Your Dynamic DNA (a.k.a. Why Do I Do That?)

Understanding who you are and how you work is an important first step in creating the life you want. Here are 5 tips to help you understand YOU:

1. Know your **learning style**. Are you visual, auditory or both? Do you learn better by touch and feel?
2. Evaluate and challenge your **beliefs** and **fears**. Are they yours, your parents', or society's? Have you tested them to see if they are true?
3. Notice your natural style or **behaviors.** Think about things that you do. Ask your friends. How do you adapt/change in different environments (work, home, etc.)?
4. Find your **passion** and **purpose**. Learn what **motivates** you. Connecting to something higher than ourselves helps us to move forward.
5. Create your **ideal surrounding**. What do YOU need to be and feel your best?

Now, you can use this information to *set yourself up for success.*

~Kricket Harrison, CPCC, ACC, PACG, Professional Coach & Speaker

Kricket Harrison, CPCC, ACC, PACG, is a Motivational Speaker & Coach who helps entrepreneurs and professionals work the way they work best. Learn more at www.BrightOutsidetheBox.com.

Chip Away All That is Not Your Highest Self with ADD Crusher

I met Alan Brown at the ACO conference this year and purchased his ADD Crusher Videos. I work with gifted college students who also have ADHD. They absolutely love the videos, do everything Alan suggests and appear to have completely turned their upside-down brilliance into laser love and learning with limitless possibility. The results were so amazing that I started mastering Alan's skills myself. Alan's ADD Crusher is the basis for my ADHD and Coaching program "Mastering your unique Brain Wiring."

~Nancy Anne Brighton, LCSW, ADHD Coach

Nancy Anne Brighton, LCSW, ADHD Coach, empowers gifted adults with upside-down brilliance to create compelling futures from the future. Bright Brains Building. Brighter Future. www.BrightONBrains.com ~ ADHDcoach@BrightonBrains.com ~ (386) 290-6703

The Sky's the Limit

Medication is not a cure. Using medication can set you up for success, but you still have to do the work to make ADHD an asset rather than a problem. It's like a novice runner who finally becomes conditioned enough to run regularly without suffering from aching legs and exhaustion afterwards. At that point, the runner is ready to do the rest of the work it takes to become a really good runner.

The good news is that people with ADHD already know how to work hard. Most people with the diagnosis have already had to work incredibly hard just to live according to societal rules. With medication, if appropriate, and tools like coaching and support groups, you can focus all that hard work on doing the things that matter, the important tasks. And from there, the sky's the limit!

~Sarah D. Wright, M.S., A.C.T.

Nationally-known ADHD coach Sarah D. Wright specializes in helping professionals in small businesses get on track and get going. FocusForEffectiveness.com ~ Sarah@FocusForEffectiveness.com (858) 408-9338.

No Loose Ends: The Last 5% of Follow-Through

Often, people with ADD will finish things 95%, and leave the final last pieces undone.

Sometimes it's that last step that makes the difference between success and failure. Maybe you completed the report but forget to send it in, missing the deadline. Or you collected information from several people for your project, but never acknowledged or thanked them... so they won't cooperate with you in the future. Or you managed to pull off a successful charity auction, but never kept notes on what worked, who did what, or the expenses and profit figures. Oops! Leaving out those final details can leave a negative impression.

There's a simple solution: Always include those final steps in your planning, putting them in the calendar. Don't consider a project complete until the loose ends are filed!

~Bonnie Mincu, MA, MBA, ADHD Coach

Bonnie Mincu, Senior Certified ADHD Coach, helps you maximize your productivity and income potential. In-depth programs on specific ADD challenges to reach your goals are available at www.thrivewithadd.com.

A Sweetheart of a Budget

If you are trying to make and keep a budget, whether with one of the many available programs and apps or by designing your own, remember KISS: Keep it Simple Sweetheart!

Many programs and books with advice about money will list various categories to describe your expenses: medical, dining out, groceries, charity, gifts, cable, electric, mortgage or rent, clothing, health club, etc. KISS means using fewer categories so it is quicker and easier to update your budget. And you will have a quick visual of where your money is going whenever you look at your budget.

So combine categories. How about using personal care for health club, clothes, dry cleaning, haircuts, etc? Gifts and charity could go together, while entertainment includes dining out, tickets you buy for events, and so on. The fewer the groups, the easier it will be.

~Abigail Wurf, M.Ed., CLC

Abigail Wurf coaches executives, entrepreneurs, couples and other adults affected by ADHD, as well as high school and college students. Available in Washington DC and nationally. awurf@verizon.net ~ www.abigailwurf.com ~ (202) 244-2234

Mental Rehearsal

When I work with clients on goal setting, one powerful tool that I use with them is visualization. There is a region in the brain that becomes activated when you visualize yourself doing something. Once this area is activated, neural pathways are formed so that you remember the thought. I am drawing from my past as a gymnast when, before physically performing any routine, I'd rehearse it in my mind first and see myself completing it successfully. The more you visualize yourself doing the same routine with success, the stronger and more established the neural pathway becomes. When setting goals, I ask my clients to visualize themselves successfully doing the action over and over. This mental rehearsal reinforces their success in reality so that when the time comes to perform, their brains are ready, willing and able.

~Dr. Billi

The AttentionB Method, Pedagogical/Class Management for ADHD with Dr. Billi, Ph.D. Tame the chaos in your classroom using my unique strategies. www.AttentionB.com ~ DrBilli@AttentionB.com ~ (855) DrBilli

Maximizing Your ADHD Entrepreneurial Brain Style

People with ADHD are 300% more likely (than those without ADHD) to be entrepreneurs. Unfortunately, only about 34% of new businesses succeed in the first five years. Two things contribute to this: 1) not maximizing our innate strengths and 2) minimizing our challenges. Maximizing our innate entrepreneurial strengths include honoring our creativity, risk-taking ability, out-of-the-box thinking and the capability to come up with extraordinary solutions. Minimizing challenges includes building competencies and strategies around less-developed areas, such as maintaining focus, attending to boring details and staying organized so you can finally pursue your passions, raise your productivity and ultimately increase your profits. Being an entrepreneur is one of the best jobs for people with ADHD, *if* you find out how to unlock the secrets to your entrepreneurial brain style!

~Laurie Dupar, PMHNP, RN, PCC, Certified ADHD Coach and Nurse Practitioner

Laurie Dupar, entrepreneur, ADHD Coach and author of *Unlock the Secrets to Your Entrepreneurial Brain Style*. Find out more at www.coachingforadhd.com or (916) 791-1799.

"Here's to the crazy ones. The misfits. The rebels. The trouble-makers. The round pegs in the square holes. The ones who see things differently. They're not fond of rules and they have no respect for the status quo. You can quote them, disagree with them, glorify, or vilify them. But the only thing you can't do is ignore them. Because they change things. They push the human race forward . And while some may see them as the crazy ones, we see genius. Because the people who are crazy enough to think they can change the world. Are the ones who do."

~ Steve Jobs

Couples & ADHD: Communication That Works!

It's easy to focus on methods of communicating that *don't* work with your particular type of ADHD. What about the methods that *do* work? From time to time, you or your partner might stumble across some method of communication that really works for you. The problem is that when communication works, we usually don't say anything. Your partner can't read your mind, so speak up and let them know what they did or said that really works for you. It can be as simple as acknowledging the tone of voice they used, the fewer words they used, how they got right to the point & didn't bring up the past, or how they focused on what *to* do instead of belaboring what *not* to do. It's empowering when you give your partner positive feedback about the specific communications they use that really work for you & your ADHD.

~ Sarah A. Ferman, L.M.F.T., P.C.C. &
Robert L. Wilford, Ph.D.

Sarah Ferman, L.M.F.T., P.C.C., & Robert Wilford, Ph.D., are leading ADHD Couples Consultants, helping ADHD Couples reconnect and create loving and enduring relationships. www.ADHDCouplesConsultants.com

Basic Rules For ADHD Medication Management

S ome rules to know about ADHD medications:

1. Know the expected DOE (Duration of Effectiveness) for any medication and discuss it with your doc.

2. Understand the side effects and how to tell when it isn't working as expected.

3. Some medications interact with other drugs you may be taking. Specific challenges are often seen with Prozac and Paxil. Just Google "CYP 450/2D6" for confirmation.

4. Look for any metabolic challenges that can cause the DOE to become unpredictable, as described in more detail in the *New ADHD Medication Rules*.

5. Both depression and anxiety can present as cognitive/thinking problems - understand the differences.

~Dr. Charles Parker

Dr. Charles Parker, Author, Neuroscience Consultant, Psychiatrist, Psychopharmacologist. About: http://bit.ly/boutcp. Teaching: CoreBrain.org. Treatment Systems: CorePsych.com. *New ADHD Medication Rules.* Amazon: http://bit.ly/ruleswork.

ADHD and the Lack of Self-Esteem

The first time Rachel (not her real name) entered my office, I thought she could easily be a model! When she mentioned to me how unattractive and stupid she was feeling, I realized how low her self-esteem was. With low self-esteem and negative self-concept often comes low aspirations and expectations which, if not reversed, could lead many individuals like Rachel to be underachievers in their professional and personal lives. The negative self-concept could be caused or worsened by inappropriate comments from parents, educators and others who are not well-informed about ADHD. Some suggestions to help your children build up their self-esteem:

- Find something they are good at and help them shine
- Have them ask to be a Teacher's Assistant (TA) in a class that is easy for them
- Ask them to guide you occasionally
- Teach them how to advocate for themselves

~Roya Kravetz, ACC, BCC, CMC

Roya Kravetz is a Board-Certified and Credentialed Life Coach/ADHD Coach and Consultant and a Certified Parent Educator. www.adhdsuccesscoaching.com ~ (858) 334-8584

Circuit Breaker for the ADHD Brain

Imagine your brain full of electricity, crackling and popping, overcharged with energy, ideas, thoughts and emotions. Wouldn't it be nice to short circuit everything that's charging through your head? The solution is nearer than you may have thought: it is one breath away.

Take a breath. Not one of those shallow breaths that start and end in your chest. A real breath: one that starts in your belly and rises up through your chest. Exhale. Notice your brain now. Is it slower, less frenetic? Do you feel like you have a grip again, even if it is for a nanosecond? Enjoy the break, even if it is momentary.

The next time everything is swirling around you, take a breath to short circuit the cycle that makes you feel overwhelmed. With practice, a few breaths can give you the relief you need and the chance to find a new perspective.

~Mindy Schwartz Katz, MS, ACC

Mindy Schwartz Katz, ADHD/Life Coach, helps ADDers get over, around and through obstacles that get in the way of living their unique life. www.yourlife-planb.com ~ mindy@yourlife-planb.com

Hints for Older ADDers

So you've decided you might have this disorder! What now? See a professional who will listen closely to your symptoms and questions and make some creative suggestions. Being an elder ADDer is quite different from being an adolescent ADDer, or even a young adult ADDer.

You will have developed bad habits over the years that will be difficult to change. On the plus side, however, you will have developed some useful strategies to deal with your disorder, without even realizing it. Many of the tips you will be offered you will already know; in fact, you may think you invented them yourself!

Most older people do not take kindly to change, but if you want to have some success harnessing your ADD, you will have to make some changes! It will be quite exciting. It will make your life much more enjoyable. Give it a chance.

~Jane Patrick, BA, MEd.

Jane Patrick, retired teacher, diagnosed with ADD at age 75. Now enjoying the trip! Advocate for neglected group of 60+ ADDers. janeham@abacom.com

A Different Kind of SMART

SMART goals are goals which fit the following criteria: S-specific; M-measureable; A-actionable; R-realistic; T-tangible.

Defining goals in this format does help. However, it takes another form of **SMART** to make success happen:

S-Systems, Strategies & Structures: Do you have a system or a strategy to help you take action toward your goal? Do you have a structure in place to keep you on track?

M-Mindset: Can you manage the negative self-talk? Can you motivate yourself to move forward?

A-Accountability: Do you have a friend, mentor, or a group to hold you accountable and provide support?

R-Routines get Results: Remember the tortoise and the hare? A steady pace wins the race.

T-Trust: Do you trust and believe in yourself & the process?

~Kricket Harrison, CPCC, ACC, PACG,
Professional Coach & Speaker

Kricket Harrison, Creator of the SMARTSuccess™ Club, an online accountability program for those who want to get things done and have more fun! www.SMARTSuccessClub.com

Radical Strategy Swap: Bigger Thinking and Smaller Doing

T*he Setup:* "I'm in the weeds, Cam!"

This is an expression heard when clients get caught in small thinking, when they get sucked down some minutia rabbit hole, like choosing the format of a spreadsheet. Or they can take too big a bite when working on a task better suited for someone with a complementary skill set.

The Swap: Think bigger, as in think more expansive. We often focus on the problem and miss the bigger opportunity. Your associative processor does better with bigger thinking, giving you access to the bigger picture.

"Doing smaller" is about honoring strength areas. We can put a premium on doing - any doing - even if we are struggling in someone else's strength area. As you cross the stream, notice the stepping stones that are more suited to your strengths and collaborate on the less savory ones.

~Cameron Gott, Trainer and Coach

Cameron Gott, PCC, a Tele-class Leader at ADDCA and developer of Curious Accountability™, partners with ADHD business owners in achieving "The Next Level." www.camerongott.com

Integrate Technology Into Your Neurology!

One adaptive strategy for ADHD or TBI is to address perceived impairments or deficits through the smart use of technology. The future has much in store for us, with technologies being developed to assist anyone with impairments, including working memory deficit, a common ADHD and TBI complaint. The use of devices such as smartphones and computers can now reduce the cognitive load on our minds, thus preserving our cognitive energy for more meaningful uses. While smartphones can be used to reduce cognitive load, some technologies and treatments are designed to increase cognitive efficiency, such as:

1. Lumosity.com
2. Neuro-feedback
3. Hyperbaric Oxygen Chamber Treatment
4. Hemispheric Integration Therapy — Functional Neurology
5. Vital Sounds Therapeutic Listening

~ Jonathan Salem, M.S.

Jonathan Salem, M.S. Specializes in Entrepreneurship, Applied Technology, and coaching clients with ADHD and/or Mild to Moderate Traumatic Brain Injury. (409) ADHD-NOW (409) 234-3669 ~ Jon@CoachADHDNow.com

Master Your Mind, Master Your Emotions and ADHD

The unique neurobiological wiring of ADHD brains creates mastery through creative intelligence, ideas, innovative solutions, inventions and high emotional intelligence. Sometimes this massive firing of emotions creates unplanned emotional explosions, overwhelm and panic. To reboot the unique operating system of the ADHD brain, remember, "Where the mind goes, energy flows."

Feel your seat and feel your feet! Moving the focus of the mind from the explosive brain to the body and grounding it by plugging the feet into mother earth creates a free flow of jet fuel for focusing on what is at hand. When the turbo fuel is grounded, thoughts truly become things.

~Nancy Anne Brighton, LCSW, ADHD Coach

Nancy Anne Brighton, LCSW, ADHD Coach, empowers gifted adults with upside-down brilliance to create compelling futures from the future. Bright Brains Building. Brighter Future. www.BrightONBrains.com ~ ADHDcoach@BrightonBrains.com ~ (386) 290-6703

Liquid Gold

An underappreciated challenge with ADHD is time awareness. This challenge is not just about telling time, but includes the difficulty of sensing or estimating the passage of time. It influences everything from planning and organizing to sensing how long 5 minutes takes or if an hour or five hours has passed.

This inability to sense the passage of time causes frequent disputes in families. Parents complain that children take too long to get out of the house, come to dinner, or get off the computer. And, conversely, that they don't spend long enough practicing, doing homework or brushing their teeth.

The answer: liquid motion timers! These timers work like an hourglass, except that their brightly colored liquid passes from one chamber to another via wheels, drips and oozes that are much more engaging. Instead of relying on a sense of time, children can actually see the time "slip" away.

~Laurie Dupar, PMHNP, RN, PCC Certified ADHD Coach and Nurse Practitioner

Laurie Dupar is an internationally-recognized expert, author and speaker on ADHD. Reach her at www.coachingforadhd.com. Find liquid timers at www.officeplayground.com.

Forget "Should"...Just Get Things Done

Doing things faster or more efficiently isn't always "better." Doing things the way that makes you comfortable is.

Don't get caught up in the "should" world. "I should do this that way because that is the way everyone else does it." Remember, doing things in a way that is uncomfortable for you increases the likelihood that the task won't get done at all. Finding ways that make sense to you and getting the job done is what really matters. How you "should" do it really doesn't.

~Abigail Wurf, M.Ed., CLC

Abigail Wurf, M.Ed., CLC coaches executives, entrepreneurs, couples and other adults affected by ADHD. Washington DC and nationally. awurf@verizon.net ~ www.abigailwurf.com ~ (202) 244-2234

Adventure vs. Perfection

Is your life a race for perfection or are you on an adventure? What's the difference? And does it have to be one or the other? Actually, yes! You see, they have completely opposite paths and results.

Perfection leads to judgment - because there is only one _right_ way to do anything – which keeps you frozen, stuck, and mired down.

On the other hand, adventure leads to choice – where there is no _wrong_ way to do anything – which leads to action and movement toward your goal.

Perfection is often the way of those with ADHD, but it doesn't have to be. Learning to make decisions and conscious choices is the key to adventure.

~Dee Shofner Doochin, MLAS, PCC, CMC, PACG, SCAC

Dee Shofner Doochin, MLAS; Professional Certified Coach; Certified Mentor Coach; Senior Certified ADHD Coach; wife, mother, grandmother, and great-grandmother with ADHD; adventurer; lover of life! www.deedoochin.com

Please Wait While Your Video Loads

Parents who don't have ADHD can find it hard to fully grasp what's happening chemically in their child's brain to cause certain behaviors. They often wonder why their child cannot sit still or wait patiently like other kids. To simplify it, I use the following demonstration. I have them log onto a video sharing site and find a video they love - something 10 minutes or longer. Inevitably, the video will play and then freeze repeatedly. It won't play properly until it catches up with the buffer time. It's the same with their child's brain; sometimes their brain is buffering due to a lack of neurochemicals, and the child cannot put the brakes on or inhibit certain behaviors until their brain chemicals catch up. So they quickly move from one thing to the other in order to stimulate their brains.

~Dr. Billi

The AttentionB Method, Pedagogical/Class Management for ADHD with Dr. Billi, Ph.D. Tame the chaos in your classroom using my unique strategies. www.AttentionB.com ~ DrBilli@AttentionB.com ~ (855) DrBilli

Puzzling Paradox: The Ongoing Dance to Fill Up & Free Up Your Time & Space

Do you find yourself constantly desperate for more free time and uncluttered space…and then inevitably fill-up any little bit of available time or space that might have been available?

...Space & time for you ...to breathe ...and just be...

~Monika Pompetzki, ADHD Coach

Monika Pompetzki, BSc, MEd, AD/HD, academic, & life coach focused on deciphering the amusing and PUZZLING PARADOXES of AD/HD. www.add-adhdCoaching.com ~ monika@add-adhdCoaching.com ~ (905) 336-8330

Radical Strategy Swap: Relax Expectations and Tighten-up on Time

The Default: It's well known that individuals with ADHD can have high expectations and struggle with the concept of time. This inverse relationship of tight or precise expectations and a looser grasp of time can be a deadly duo, standing in the way of consistent completion.

The Swap: With expectations, notice your aim for the "keyhole" when the "doorway" is perfectly acceptable. Relaxing and making expectations less precise leaves room for success to show up in different ways. With respect to time, notice if its relative value swings dramatically. Hours before a deadline, time is the most valuable thing imagined. Yet weeks before a deadline, it's wholesaled, given away freely. One way to tighten our concept of time is to assign a more consistent monetary value (say, $50) to every hour, regardless of when it occurs.

~Cameron Gott, Trainer and Coach

Cameron Gott, PCC, a Tele-class Leader at ADDCA and developer of Curious Accountability™, partners with ADHD business owners in achieving "The Next Level." www.camerongott.com

Tips to Lick Your Impulsive Speech

Impulsivity is a common ADHD symptom that often leads to speaking before thinking - sometimes in anger, sometimes in hurt and pain, and sometimes in frustration. Learn to count to ten, breathe, and slow your response down (only takes a few seconds).

A great tool for my clients is the acronym TAXI:

T - For Trigger (something triggers you!);

A - Acknowledge that you are triggered and identify your feelings;

X - eXhale; and

I - I *choose* to act/react differently.

TAXI can alleviate many situations which result in hurt, discouragement and anger between spouses. Try it; you'll see great results!

~Sherry Clarke, MA, LCMFT, ACG

Sherry Clarke, MA, LCMFT, a veteran Licensed Marriage and Family Therapist and ADHD Coach, has a passion for helping couples and parents understand, embrace and celebrate their ADHD. www.clarkecoaching.com

Focus or Clarity, Which Comes First?

"If I could only focus, I could get clear."

Imagine a crystal ball—like in a fairy tale. The premise is that by gazing (focusing) on the ball, you will clearly see what you are searching for: the future, the answer, or even home sweet home. Now imagine this crystal ball is covered in dust and soot. *No matter how hard you focus on the ball, you won't see the message clearly.* Therefore, you spend your time focusing on the dirt instead of the message the crystal ball is trying to show.

You see, **clarity** is an understanding of what is wanted, needed, a desired outcome. **Focus** is where you put your attention to reach that outcome. If you're not clear on where to direct your focus, action won't happen. Get clear on what you need to focus on; don't focus on what you need to get clear on.

~Kricket Harrison, CPCC, ACC, PACG, Professional Coach & Speaker

Kricket Harrison, Certified Professional Coach & Speaker, helps people with too many ideas get clear, take action and move forward. www.BrightOutsidetheBox.com

"Distracted, Disorganized or ADD?"

Isn't everyone distracted at some time? Doesn't everyone forget things, or act a bit impulsively? Aren't we all ADD? Yes, everyone's forgetful or distracted on occasion...now and then. The difference is that people with ADHD experience it so consistently that it creates ongoing problems in their lives. It negatively and consistently affects their academics, work or social relationships. The key to knowing if you have ADHD is that it has existed since childhood and has persisted throughout your life. To know the difference between "normal" distraction and ADHD, ask yourself if your inattention, disorganization, and the inability to complete tasks are at the same level as that of your peers. Is it more problematic? Do you struggle more? If so, you might want to see your doctor about the possibility of having ADHD.

~Laurie Dupar, PMHNP, RN, PCC, Certified ADHD Coach and Nurse Practitioner

Laurie Dupar, PMHNP, RN, PCC, is a trained psychiatric mental health nurse practitioner and certified ADHD coach. You can find out more at www.coachingforadhd.com.

Move to Pay Better Attention

How often are we told to sit still and pay attention? The notion seems to be that distractions keep you from focusing and that focusing on a single thing is the best way to learn. It turns out that movement actually helps people learn and increases their ability to recall. In one study, students from a traditional learning environment were asked to observe and recall landmarks on a map. Students who viewed the map from multiple perspectives remembered more landmarks and locations than students who viewed the map from a single perspective. The students with ADHD who were allowed to move while observing and memorizing those landmarks, did better than all the rest.* So, let yourself and your children move. It helps your brains work better!

*Carson, S., Shih, M., Langer, E. (2001). Sit Still and Pay Attention? *Journal of Adult Development*, Vol. 8, No.3, 183-188.

~Roland Rotz, Ph.D. & Sarah D. Wright, M.S.

Roland Rotz, Ph.D., and Sarah D. Wright, M.S., are authors of *Fidget to Focus*, a handbook of strategies for living more easily with ADHD. www.FidgetToFocus.com

"Trust yourself. You know more than you think you do."

~ Dr. Spock

3 Simple Ways to Reduce Interruptions from Others

Minimizing interruptions from others is critical for effective time management. Try these three simple ways to reduce interruptions:

1. Develop a code word. It can even be fun to choose something silly to let others know you are doing focused work and cannot be interrupted. For example, if you have a home office and your child interrupts you, say "watermelon" to signal that you are doing focused work. (Be sure to explain this ahead of time!)

2. Use a sign outside your cubicle or office to let co-workers know that there is "focused work in progress" so they know not to interrupt you.

3. The phone can be a big interruption source. When doing focused work, either silence your ringer or go to a quiet space like a conference room or library. Manage interruptions to make the best use of your valuable time.

~Laura Rolands, ADHD Coach

Laura Rolands is an ADHD Coach who helps clients manage time, reduce interruptions, focus on priorities, increase productivity and achieve goals. Learn more at www.MyAttentionCoach.com.

R-E-S-P-E-C-T

Teenagers with ADHD are struggling to mature, to become adults. This is not an easy process as many of their emotions are immature, yet the need for independence progresses. There is one word that is the most powerful at this point in their lives: RESPECT. Their increased value of respect is an integral part of a teen's passage to independence and the yearning to make their own decisions. Giving respect means showing their value by involving them in family decision making, speaking to them as an adult, recognizing their needs and discussing their issues, showing consideration for their correct choices, and voicing appreciation. Respect is important to support a teen toward maturity. Treating and speaking to your teen with respect is the most important thing you can do. They will demand it from you if you don't give it to them. It is an equation: give respect = get respect; give disrespect = get disrespect.

~Judith Champion, MSW, ACG

Judith Champion, MSW, ACG, ADHD Family Coach and Educator. ADHD affects the whole family. Coaching for parents, children and adults. www.ADHDAssociates.com ~ (609) 468-0819 judith@judithchampion.com

Hammers & Screws

It doesn't take much carpentry training to know you need the right tools for any job. No matter how hard you hammer a screw, you're not going to get the results you want. You might eventually pound the screw into the wood, but it won't hold. There are times in life when we need the right tools to solve problems. If your job requires reports or paperwork to be completed within specific deadlines, you need a system to keep up with what needs to be done and when. If not, you'll always be missing deadlines and scrambling like you're running on ice, slipping and falling but never getting anywhere. Einstein said, "Insanity is doing the same thing and expecting different results." If the hammer isn't working, find a screwdriver. If you don't have a screwdriver, find someone who does: a coach, friend, or mentor, anyone who can help you find a screwdriver. You owe it to yourself.

~Rose Smith, M. Ed.

Rose Smith, M. Ed. For more helpful hints and random reflections, please visit http://RandomReflectionsbyRose.wordpress.com/.

Medication Increases Awareness in Relationships

O ften, when adults begin ADHD medication for the first time, they notice troublesome things in their relationships or their work environment. Those things may have always been there! Medication heightens awareness and motivation. The first step is noticing what feels different, and then taking action. Remember, one issue at a time and one day at a time. Get clear about what you are working on since you cannot tackle them all at once. Set powerful intentions for what you DO want for your future. Share those goals with others and give yourself time to adjust to the new you. Significant change is not always comfortable.

~Lisa Boester, ADHD Coach

Lisa Boester is a Professionally Trained ADHD Life Coach and Consultant. She has a diverse family of clients from business owners to homemakers to other coaches. (317) 879-6457 lbboester@gmail.com ~ www.adhdartoflife.com

Unearth Your Student's Inner Brilliance Today to Inspire Later

Exhume your student's buried talents to make things interesting! For example: A teen client, an amazing artist, was struggling with physiology in high school. He hated reading, struggled to learn all the "systems" in the body, and his GPA was suffering an untimely death! His mother was completely unstable. As we talked, I saw him sketching. He was supposed to be studying the "circulatory system." So I asked, "Why don't you draw it?" He looked puzzled. "Draw a transparent person. Why not?" I said. He said, "We could see his heart pumping, his veins and arteries bulging, right?"

"Right!" Was my response. "Use colors, such as red for arteries like the aorta, blue for veins to show blood." His imagination skyrocketed! Now the class was interesting! In the end, he created "characters" for each of the "systems" of the body and received an "A" in the class.

~Sandy Alletto Corbin, MA, ACG, SCAC

Sandy Alletto Corbin, a Senior Credentialed ADHD Coach and teacher, woman with ADHD and a single mother of an ADHD daughter, specializes in coaching women, teens and college students and advocating for change. www.lifecoachsandyalletto.com

Change Your Language: Say "After" Instead of "If"

Subtle tweaks of language can have a powerful impact. We all know the power of magic words like "please" and "thank you." Well, there are lots of magic words out there that can make a huge difference in how people, especially our kids, respond to us. One of our favorites is the word "after" instead of the word "if." Think about it. "After you brush your teeth." "After you do your homework." "After you give me a hug and a kiss." So often we get caught up in the "if...then" of negotiation with our kids, which only puts them on the defensive. "If you do your homework, then..." just leaves a kid begging to say out loud, "Well, what if I don't? Huh? What then?" So try to use "after..." and see what comes next. Want to really throw them off? Try "Yes, of course, after..." Nothing like a little affirmation to really confuse kids into doing what you've asked!

~ Elaine Taylor-Klaus, CPCC, ACC, and
Diane Dempster, MHSA, CPC, ACC

ImpactADHD helps parents help kids. Elaine Taylor-Klaus & Diane Dempster provide reality-based training, with coaching to make it stick. We help your family thrive! http://www.ImpactADHD.com

Moving Forward by Tracking Backwards

To beat back overwhelm during periods when nothing on your to-do list seems to get done, try it "backwards." Instead of listing what you *intend* to do, record what you just did. Number each item. Then, cross them out – just as you would if you wrote today's list yesterday. At the end of the day you'll have a long list of "done's."

Give yourself credit for every teensy thing you do and notice what it does to your mood and activation level. You'll probably find yourself doing more just to have a longer list, but more is *not* the goal; avoid such pressures that may shut you down! The backwards to-do list works because most brains subconsciously link cross-outs with completion. Completions release neurochemicals that make us feel more effective and give us the impetus to remain in action with intentionality. Action begets action! Counter-intuitive, but it usually works. Try it.

~Madelyn Griffith-Haynie, CTP, CMC, A.C.T.

Madelyn Griffith-Haynie, global ADD expert, multi-certified coaching pioneer, ADD coaching field co-founder, brain-based trainer, neuro-diversity advocate, and speaker, helps clients turn *can't* to *competence*. mgh@addcoach.com ~ www.ADDandSoMuchMore.com

Change the Perspective

A diagnosis of ADHD can bring a good deal of anxiety with it. We think it makes us different, broken. But remember, "normal" people aren't studied, precisely because they are normal. People outside the norm, those diagnosed with ADHD for example, are studied. This means there are "instruction manuals" and experts that can help those with ADHD work within the framework provided by their unique brains. That's an advantage. "Regular" people often have to flail around blindly, trying figure out how to maximize their strengths and minimize their weaknesses. For those of us with ADHD, much of that work is already done. All you have to do is go looking for it. (Which you're clearly already doing if you're reading this, so kudos to you!)

~Brendan Mahan, M.Ed.

Brendan Mahan, M.Ed. is an ADHD coach specializing in helping students with ADHD and their families find success in school and at home. mahancoaching@gmail.com.

What Do You Do When Your Internal Clock Is Broken?

Insomnia is great if you love late-night TV, but the increase in ADHD symptoms isn't worth catching the monologues. Here are several tools to help people with delayed sleep disorders reset their natural sleep cycle:

• Light Therapy: get 30 minutes of natural light with an American Academy of Sleep Medicine-approved device between 6 a.m. - 8 a.m. every morning

• Filters: use screen filters or software, such as f.lux, to control blue light emissions from computer/tablet screens

• Melatonin: take 4-6 hours before bed every evening

• Dim Light: schedule 45 minutes of light levels below 65 lux about 1-2 hours before bed

• Digital Video Recorder: late-night one-liners are just as funny in the daytime

Make sure to get an eye exam and consult a sleep specialist or physician before beginning light therapy or melatonin.

~Sunny Aldrich, Professional ADHD Coach

Sunny Aldrich is the first professional ADHD Coach in Alaska. She specializes in emotional procrastination, ADHD strength assessment, dyslexia, and homeschooling. http://www.adhdpower.com ~ sunny@adhdpower.com.

Picture the Reward

There is strong evidence that suggests a connection between ADHD and eating disorders. Being overweight and in poor health is more difficult for people with ADHD, since it's no secret that motivation is one of the keys to losing weight and staying healthy. For people with ADHD, who generally lack motivation, one of the greatest techniques to getting and staying motivated is to connect the reward with the goal. A tip I give my clients is to hang a picture on the refrigerator when they were at a healthy weight and liked how they looked. If they can't find one, I have them edit a current one to a healthier, slimmer version of themselves. I have them mark down every time they resisted opening the fridge. The picture helps them visualize the reward of losing weight and also visually connects the motivation to the goal of eating healthier and exercising.

~Dr. Billi

The AttentionB Method, Pedagogical/Class Management for ADHD with Dr. Billi, Ph.D. Tame the chaos in your classroom using my unique strategies. www.AttentionB.com ~ DrBilli@AttentionB.com ~ (855) DrBilli

Stay on Task: Do What You're Doing

Staying on a task, not getting distracted from it. Impossible for the ADDer? Nah. The trick is LABELING. You need 3 LABELS:

1) What I'm Doing Now
2) BS That I'm NOT Doing Now
3) Important But NOT What I'm Doing Now

Create these labels in your mind - with color, size and shape - and stick on tasks/thoughts/things. Decide the ONE task you want to focus on and LABEL it "What I'm Doing Now." When engaged in that important task, distractions arise. If not important, LABEL them as "BS That I'm NOT Doing Now." Then go back to "What I'm Doing Now."

If an interruption comes that you can't just swat away, fine: LABEL it "Important But NOT What I'm Doing Now," and make a note. Then return to "What I'm Doing Now!"

~Alan Brown

Alan Brown, a struggling exec until diagnosed with ADD, crafted the success strategies in ADD Crusher™ videos -- interactive tools helping ADDers live to their potential. www.ADDCrusher.com

Couples & ADHD: Building Trust in 3 Steps

Keeping your promises cements the trust that builds strong relationships. Here are three simple tips for the partner with ADHD to build trust in their relationship:

1. Pick your promises carefully. Before saying "yes," ask yourself if it is something you have time for and are willing and capable of doing. The secret is to not over-promise when you can't deliver.

2. Protect your promises by creating back-up systems. Saying "yes" means taking action to remember your promise. Set an alarm, use a giant note on the door, whatever it takes to protect your promise.

3. Manage your partner's expectations. Setting a target time to deliver on your promise helps you stay timely, manages your partner's expectations, and allows you to keep your promise.

~ Sarah A. Ferman, L.M.F.T., P.C.C.
& Robert L. Wilford, Ph.D.

Sarah Ferman, L.M.F.T., P.C.C., & Robert Wilford, Ph.D., are leading ADHD Couples Consultants, helping ADHD Couples reconnect and create loving and enduring relationships. www.ADHDCouplesConsultants.com

Make Learning Easier with a Simple Brain Exercise

Here's a brain exercise to help you learn and focus, and a brief explanation about how it works. A brain chemical called dopamine helps you learn, plan, and make decisions. This exercise uses eye movements to strengthen the dopamine-producing parts of your brain in a natural way, and help you stay on track when you need to.

Hold your two thumbs one inch apart and about eight inches in front of your face. Look back and forth, one thumb to the other, two times. Now move your thumbs to a new position and repeat. With each new position, hold your thumbs an inch apart, while you make one thumb closer to your face than the other and one thumb higher than the other. Mix it up with a variety of thumb positions. Watch a video demonstration of this and other brain-building exercises to help ADHD and Learning Disabilities at www.BrainTimeVideos.com.

~ Dr. Jim Otis, Fellow, American College of Functional Neurology

Dr. Otis specializes in drug-free treatment for ADHD and Learning Disabilities and is the inventor of BrainTime™, a patent-pending technology for optimal brain health. www.BrainTimeVideos.com

What Causes ADHD?

Having accurate information is one of the most effective ways to succeed with ADHD. So I wanted to answer the popular question, "What causes ADHD?" with a few facts:

• A single cause for ADHD has not been proven yet.

• Studies show that people with ADHD have a lower amount of certain neurotransmitters active in their brains.

• Other theories include damage, trauma, bacterial infection, viral infection or metal intoxication to the brain, which may cause a small percentage of ADHD symptoms.

• Some people believe food allergies cause ADHD. Food allergies may account for 3% of people with ADHD; however, allergies alone do not account for most people with ADHD symptoms.

Research suggests the strongest cause for ADHD is genetics. If a child has ADHD, there's a 30%-40% chance the biological parents have ADHD.

~Laurie Dupar, PMHNP, RN, PCC, Certified ADHD Coach and Nurse Practitioner

Laurie Dupar, PMHNP, RN, PCC, is a trained psychiatric mental health nurse practitioner and certified ADHD coach. You can find out more at www.coachingforadhd.com.

You CAN Judge a Book by Its Cover

Is that Harry Potter Collection simply too much to get your brain wrapped around? In spite of the lure of adventure, magic and intrigue, might picking up one book condemn you to an overwhelmed state? This fear was the case for one bright 8-year-old girl. She so wanted to be like her friends whom had jumped aboard the Hogwarts Express. Reading assignments for school also left her in a stare-down with many a book cover. A small paper clip solved her big problem. In her low-key, yet brilliant manner, she simply decided how many pages she could read and slid the clip on the last of those pages. This action left her with a manageable amount of reading during any one sitting with the book. Nothing after that paper clip existed until SHE decided. Open and shut case.

~Nancy Bean, Certified ADHD Coach,
Professional Organizer, Interior Designer

Nancy Bean builds relationships between people, places and spaces, helping clients create change in their lives. SIMPLIFY by DESIGN: Certified ADHD Coach, Designer/Organizer. simplify@nancybean.com

What Would You Attempt To Do If You Knew You Could Not Fail?

R ead the question out loud:

What would I try to do if I knew I could not fail?

- Sit for a few minutes and allow your mind to wander.
- You might want to make a list of the things that come to your mind.
- When looking at the list or just thinking about it, what does that look and feel like? In as much detail as possible.
- What will it mean for you to achieve this?
- How will achieving this goal be in alignment with who you truly are?

If this has inspired you to want to achieve anything, you can ask a friend or family member for support, or you might want to find a trained ADHD coach who can help you create an action plan and support you all the way to your success.

You can do it. Go for it!

~Charlotte Hjorth, ADHD Coach, PCC

Charlotte Hjorth, Certified ADHD Coach, PCC - Supervisor, Trainer, Speaker, Writer and Blogger - Initiator and Campaign Leader of ADHD Awareness Week Denmark since 2008. www.ADHDkompagniet.com

ADHD Medication Dosage Absolutely Matters

Many ask: "What is the biggest problem you see with stimulant medications?" That answer wraps up easily into one simple word: dosage.

Many other problems can occur with the complexity of biomedical challenges associated with treating executive function problems; last time I checked, the body was connected with the mind. How does the dosage problem reveal itself? Watch carefully for the *Therapeutic Window* and *Duration of Effectiveness* [DOE]. Customization for every single med and for every person is the answer.

The key is simple: know your dosing strategies, work with your doc to customize the dose, know what is expected, and become active in the process. Your doc can't get those meds right without your participation, your knowledge, and your help.

~Dr. Charles Parker

Dr Charles Parker, Author, Neuroscience Consultant, Psychiatrist, Psychopharmacologist. About: http://bit.ly/boutcp. Teaching: CoreBrain.org. Treatment Systems: CorePsych.com. *ADHD Medication Rules*. Amazon: http://bit.ly/ruleswork.

Try a Little Empathy

Parenting a child with ADHD is likely the hardest job you might ever have - more so if you have ADHD, as well. A little empathy goes a long way in the heat of the moment. If you are this frustrated watching your child do (or not do) something, imagine how it feels to actually be in his or her shoes. Trying to understand (or remember) how it feels to fail, yet again, might help you step back a bit and choose the best response. A smile of understanding, a gentle hug or some words of encouragement can do wonders for your child - and you!

For more on this topic, go to www.FocusForEffectiveness.com/blog.

~Roxanne Fouche, ADHD Coach

Roxanne Fouche, ADHD Coach, helps both students and women live successfully with ADHD and related challenges. In person, phone, or Skype. Contact (858) 484-4749 or Roxanne@FocusForEffectiveness.com.

Don't Give Up Your Dreams: See Time and Persevere

My client knew she needed help. She needed to complete a project to get her Master's Degree in order to pursue a new career. Being an older woman with a recent diagnosis of ADHD, she felt lost as to how she should proceed. I gave her external tools like a timer and sticky notes. We had weekly coaching sessions and I helped her break the project into steps. We set goals and daily plans.

When we started, she was completely overwhelmed because the project requirements were very complex. It was no wonder that she was stuck and frustrated! Over the months we worked together, she got better at using her time. She carried her timer with her constantly. It was a challenging experience but she never considered quitting. She kept a positive 'can do' attitude to reach her goal. It just took understanding the tools she needed, coaching support, and lots of energy. She did it!

~Dr. Laurie Senders, Ph.D.

Laurie Senders, Ph.D., Certified Life Coach, ADHD Coach, and a diagnosed ADHD adult. Learn more about Laurie and her transformational coaching at www.CompellingADHDCoach.com.

Pounce on Small Problems ... Avoid Big Challenges

In business, you can't afford to under-respond to a problem. Small problems have a way of spiraling out of control and becoming big challenges. For example, if you wait too long to address the legitimate concerns of a key employee, you may risk that employee deciding you'll never really address the problem and bolting to your competition. That loss could cause you all kinds of headaches.

Challenges that are ignored, or take too long to resolve, can threaten your most important goals. Instead of under-responding, bring out your big guns and go after problems quickly. Make solving them a top priority. Over-respond to small problems so you won't have big challenges to deal with.

~Paul O'Connor, MCC

Paul O'Connor coaches business executives with ADHD. He is a Master Certified Coach, secretary of the Professional Association of ADHD Coaches, based in Atlanta. (404) 377-4712 paul@EnergyForLifeCoach.com ~ www.EnergyForLifeCoach.com

"People rarely succeed unless they are having fun at what they are doing."

~ Dale Carnegie

S.W.E.E.P. It Up!

U se this acronym for 5 major executive functions of the brain to notice where you might be getting stuck or need some support. What action can you take to build up those areas? Also, observe your strengths and continue to nurture them!

Self-talk: that internalized language which guides behaviors and actions

Working memory and recall: holding, accessing and integrating stored facts

Emotions: involves internal regulating, tolerance, ability to control before acting or speaking

Effort and arousal: needed to activate, sustain attention and complete tasks

Problem solving: the complex act of manipulating an issue, breaking it apart and re-organizing components into useful, productive ideas.

~Melissa Fahrney, M.A., CPC

Melissa Fahrney, certified ADHD Coach & School Psychologist in Montana, specializes in heart-centered coaching for young people.... "Don't Stress Out, Strengthen Within." www.addheartworks.com ~ (888) 327-5727

"A goal without a plan is just a wish." Antoine de Saint Exupery

Even though I know better, my ADHD sometimes gets in the way of my goals. My brain wants to jump in and take off, but often I can't really get started. It finally hit me that I need to stop and plan before I will act. Recently, I wanted to start a complimentary twenty-minute consultation service for new clients. It was in my head but I did not know how to start, so I didn't. Weeks went by. My coach helped me to put a plan to paper. As some wise man said, "Don't think it, ink it." That was the key to get me moving to make my goal a reality. I have found that coaching helps my brain do some of its best thinking.

~Dr. Laurie Senders

Dr. Laurie Senders, Life and ADHD Coach. Transforms women entrepreneurs into well-organized, time-oriented, money-producing people. drlsenders@comcast.net

Note to Self: Stop Interrupting Me!

Interruptions + ADHD = difficult combination. Interruptions cause lost focus, and transitioning back to work takes significant time with ADHD. Some of the most common interruptions are self-interruptions, such as when we are working on a task and a thought regarding another task interrupts us. To reduce self-interruptions, first try keeping track of them in a notebook.

Ask yourself:
1. What was the interruption?
2. Why did it happen now?
3. How can I avoid it in the future?

To further address self-interruptions, chunk your time. Tell yourself you'll focus on this one thing for 15 minutes, and then turn away from common distractions like your computer. Work up to longer chunks of time as you experience success. If you can reduce the number of times you interrupt yourself, you will increase your productivity.

~Laura Rolands, ADHD Coach

Laura Rolands is an ADHD Coach who helps clients manage time, reduce interruptions, focus on priorities, increase productivity and achieve goals. Learn more at www.MyAttentionCoach.com.

Couples & ADHD: Winding Down or Heating Up

Shutting off your mind at night and getting a good night's sleep can be a real struggle when you have ADHD. At night, when the world is quiet, the ADHD brain's "stimulation-seeking radar" spins even faster, looking for anything to remain engaged. This makes it difficult for the ADHD brain to wind down in the evening, making it a prime time for your brain to reawaken itself by encouraging a verbal dispute with your partner. Arguing and fighting before bed is very activating, and it interferes with the process of getting a good night's sleep.

We encourage our ADHD couples to agree that in the hour before bedtime, they refrain from serious inquiries and "hot" topics. Since the ADHD brain self-medicates with conflict as the "wind down" approaches, we suggest keeping a notepad on the nightstand to easily jot down questions and discussions better held for the next day.

~ Sarah A. Ferman, L.M.F.T., P.C.C.
& Robert L. Wilford, Ph.D.

Sarah Ferman, L.M.F.T., P.C.C., & Robert Wilford, Ph.D., are leading ADHD Couples Consultants, helping ADHD Couples reconnect and create loving and enduring relationships. www.ADHDCouplesConsultants.com

ADHD: A Global Community

"How common is ADHD?" is a frequent question I get when I speak to audiences about ADHD. The answer might surprise you, considering that there seem to be some people that propose that ADHD is being over-diagnosed, not only in the United States but in other English-speaking countries. Despite what some want to believe, scientific research and studies show, over and over again, that ADHD affects, conservatively, about 3-5% of the world's population. It affects people on every continent and in every culture, all over the globe. ADHD does not discriminate based on ethnic background or if you are male or female. Equal numbers of boys/girls and men/women have ADHD. Whether you are Caucasian, African-American, Asian, Hispanic, etc., ADHD does not discriminate. Welcome to our world!

~Laurie Dupar, PMHNP, RN, PCC, Certified ADHD Coach and Nurse Practitioner

Laurie Dupar, PMHNP, RN, PCC, is a trained psychiatric mental health nurse practitioner and certified ADHD coach. You can find out more at www.coachingforadhd.com.

Forget Perfect and Get a Life

Forget perfect; settle for good enough on most things and free yourself.

Save perfect for what you love. You will have the time now!

~Abigail Wurf, M.Ed., CLC

Abigail Wurf coaches executives, entrepreneurs, couples and other adults affected by ADHD, as well as high school and college students. Serving Washington DC and nationally.
awurf@verizon.net ~ www.abigailwurf.com ~ (202) 244-2234

Warming Your Engine

You know how sometimes you really have to do something and just can't seem to get started or get in the right frame of mind to do it? Commit to "warming your engine." Put in a 15-minute good faith effort on the task.

Time it!

More than likely, you'll find that by the end of that warm-up period, you're going full steam ahead.

If you're still not in gear, go do something else for a while. But remember, it's easy to put off things that feel difficult to do. So before you quit, name the time you'll come back. Then try again later.

~Sarah D. Wright, M.S., A.C.T.

Nationally-known ADHD coach Sarah D. Wright specializes in helping professionals in small businesses get on track and get going. FocusForEffectiveness.com ~ Sarah@FocusForEffectiveness.com (858) 408-9338.

Peace of Place Helps Peace of Mind

Quieting down your brain can power it up. And a quiet mind is easier in a quiet, clean space. Peace of mind is aided by peace of place.

Stress puts our ADHD in charge. And we add stress with a cluttered desk or room, thanks to the visual noise plus the reminder of chronic non-finishing of things!

You don't have to empty out the house. All you need - at least to start - is one place of peace, where you can "shut up your mind." Space for a comfy chair. Or a small part of your home to de-clutter, keep visually quiet. Or start with just your desk.

When whooped by mind-cluttering BS or a tough project, go there. You'll find renewed energy, if you allow your mind to get quiet. Think about the mental peace when taking in a blue sky or the surface of a lake. Make the surfaces you live with more like that!

~Alan Brown

Alan Brown, a struggling exec until diagnosed with ADD, crafted the success strategies in ADD Crusher™ videos: interactive tools helping ADDers live to their potential. www.ADDCrusher.com

The CEO in Your Brain

A great way to explain how your executive functions work is to imagine an executive sitting at a big mahogany executive desk in your prefrontal cortex (where your executive functions are housed). On the executive's desk are two boxes: an IN box and an OUT box. Now, this executive is very smart and very capable but can only work on information that is delivered to his/her IN box. Here is the bugaboo of ADHD: the neurotransmitters, largely dopamine and norepinephrine, that are instrumental in bringing the information to the executive's desk do not function properly. So the very capable executive is left with nothing to do, leaving the body's response system in the hands of the amygdale, the reactive part of the brain. Our goal is to find ways to get the information to the executive so he/she can capably handle the situation.

~ Alan R. Graham, Ph.D., PCC, SCAC

Alan R. Graham, Ph.D., PCC, SCAC, trains ADD coaches for Mentorcoach, coaches executives with business and organizational challenges, and works with ADHD adults, teens, children and parents. www.ADDvisor.com ~ (847) 824-1235

Dopamine and Productivity Booster - Start off with a Fun Thing!

Conventional time management experts teach us to attack our to-do list by finishing the most urgent and important tasks first. For an interest-based brain such as that of many entre- and intrapreneurs, this strategy could be counterproductive and instead shut down the whole system, because of overwhelm or boredom. Instead, consider the opposite: start with a fun task to get you going. Interest stimulates your brain and boosts the dopamine level, which enhances the communication between your brain's reward system and the prefrontal cortex. Simply put, it makes things happen. This will then create a momentum to help you move down your to-do list.

~Anna Maria Lindell

Anna Maria Lindell, ADDCA graduate. Helping entre- and intrapreneurs to increase productivity. Co-founder of the ACO Global Expansion Committee. www.facebook.com/advancesweden.se ~ www.advancesweden.se

Don't Leave Your Desk Without Your Notepad!

Do you work in an environment where you're likely to get stopped at any time with a direction, a to-do, or a question to follow up on? If you're relying on remembering to get back to the person, or to get the item right, you're asking for trouble. And if you're stopped in the hall on the way to somewhere else, you may feel awkward asking the person who stopped you to wait while you write down what they said.

A safe strategy is to simply always have a notepad and pen with you, even if you're on the way to the restroom. Then you can take down what you're told, without stressing out about remembering.

Of course, you'll then need to DO something with that note you made once you get back to your desk. So make it a habit of looking at your notepad before you sit back down.

~Bonnie Mincu, MA, MBA, ADHD Coach

Bonnie Mincu, Senior Certified ADHD Coach, helps you maximize your productivity and income potential. In-depth programs on specific ADD challenges to reach your goals are available at www.thrivewithadd.com.

Radical Strategy Swap: Look Inward on Self-Care and Look Outward on Finishing Projects

The Default: Those of us with ADHD can be such external animals. When addressing one's needs, we often look outward, taking care of others around us and putting ourselves last. Conversely, when we get close to a deadline we tend to look inward, putting our heads down and pushing the project over the finish line, without utilizing resources around us.

The Swap: Often, we don't access others' skill sets to help finish a project because in our mind, it's too late and we can be embarrassed to ask for help. Earlier in the process, look outward and identify resources that can help with the last 10% of the project at hand.

When it comes to addressing one's needs, try looking inward first. I love my colleague Kate Kelly's expression, "put your oxygen mask on first."

~Cameron Gott, Trainer and Coach

Cameron Gott, PCC, a Tele-class Leader at ADDCA and developer of Curious Accountability™, partners with ADHD business owners in achieving "The Next Level." www.camerongott.com

Survival Tips for ADHD

Some tips to help you **enjoy life and get the best of it**:

- Learn about your ADHD - Be your own best advocate.
- Focus on your strengths - Accept and work on your challenges.
- Use your energy to change the things that fuel your energy – Leave the rest.
- Remember your successes – Write them in a Success Diary.
- Stop hiding – Start seeing yourself as the unique person you really are.
- Stop trying to fit in – Be true to yourself.
- Learn to pause – Breathe deeply while counting to 10.
- Relationships either strengthen us or weaken us – Choose yours wisely.
- Whatever you focus on grows – Make sure to nourish your mind with positive thoughts.
- Perfection is an illusion – Doing your best is good enough.
- Failure doesn't exist, there is only experience – Use it as feedback.
- Accept reality - Accept yourself - Accept life!

~Charlotte Hjorth, ADHD Coach, PCC

Charlotte Hjorth, Certified ADHD Coach, PCC - Supervisor, Trainer, Speaker, Writer and Blogger - Initiator and Campaign Leader of ADHD Awareness Week Denmark since 2008. www.ADHDkompagniet.com

Daily Tune-up with the Dynamic Duo: Intentions and Gratitude

I am convinced that setting daily intentions and listing the things we are grateful for creates forward movement. Get yourself a notebook and set aside 5 minutes a day in the a.m. or p.m. to do this powerful combination. It is amazing to see the things we set as intentions show up as quickly as the following day. Keep persistent with your intentions. Repetition is like magic. Practicing daily gratitude helps shift you in to a more positive mood. There is always something to be grateful for. I recommend five intentions and five things you are grateful for each day. If you can't come up with that many, start with one or two and build up. When positive things start happening, you will feel energized by all the movement!

~Cindy Diaz, ACC, ACG, Life Coach

Cindy Diaz, ACC, ACG, Power of Intention Coaching, Certified Life Coach specializing in ADHD. www.powerofintentioncoaching.com ~ (707) 579-2433 ~ cindylee@sonic.net

"Success will never be a big step in the future, but a small step taken now."

~Jonaton Martensson

An ADHD Conundrum

Why are stimulants used when someone is hyperactive? This is one of ADHD's biggest brainteasers! You see, the physical hyperactivity seen in some persons with ADHD is actually a symptom of inactivity of the brain. When people are moving about, restless, the physical movement of the body helps to increase the amount of dopamine available to the brain.

Not enough dopamine getting to the front part of the brain is the main problem thought to cause ADHD. Without full access to this part of the brain responsible for executive function, the ability to pay attention, focus on things less interesting, stop before we act, etc., is nearly impossible. It's a bit like expecting someone with a vision problem to simply "focus" so that they can see better; not happening!

~Laurie Dupar, PMHNP, RN, PCC, Certified ADHD Coach and Nurse Practitioner

Laurie Dupar, PMHNP, RN, PCC, is a trained psychiatric mental health nurse practitioner and certified ADHD coach. You can find out more at www.coachingforadhd.com.

Bin There, Done That!

It's amazing how items tend to sprout feet and wander into rooms where they don't belong, especially if you have children (or co-workers). Unfortunately, those same items never manage to walk themselves back where they came from, and one frustrated coaching client continually found himself, in every room but his kitchen, distracted by things he came across while escorting the "runaways" back to their respective homes. To avoid this dilemma, put several bins, boxes or other containers on the floor or just outside the door of the room you are cleaning. Place items destined for the same room in one container. For example, one box is for garage items, one for bathroom items and one for bedroom items. Once the first room is clean you can take the bins with you to the next room until all the rooms are clean and the bins are empty.

~Sunny Aldrich, Professional ADHD Coach

Sunny Aldrich is the first professional ADHD Coach in Alaska. She specializes in emotional procrastination, ADHD strength assessment, dyslexia, and homeschooling. http://www.adhdpower.com ~ sunny@adhdpower.com.

State Real Needs Firmly & They Will Adjust

Adults and children with ADHD act with the assumption that others will comply with their requests. When their requests are not met, they get furious. Most of the time, they make plans without confirming with others. They do not want to face any obstacles on their way.

Parents, teachers and spouses of ADHD people, if you want to live comfortably and also let your ADHD loved ones live peacefully with others, be sure to acknowledge your own needs and stay firm with your decisions. Remember those with ADHD can get angry easily and experience mood swings. It is better to have small conflicts initially rather than bigger ones later on. Do not judge them or create a big fuss out of their actions. Just let them deal with their rage. With practice, they will learn to organize themselves. A diagnosed and informed person will understand that his/her anger is caused by ADHD and will calm down after a while.

~Suzan Tana Alalu, MA, ACC, PACG

Suzan Tana Alalu, MA in Psychology and Expressive Arts, ACC, Professional ADHD Coach in Turkey, specializes in transforming your attention and relationship systems. talalu@dehbka.com

Helpful Computer Tips

I am getting ready to start my own business.

Until I can get a business computer, I have set up a desktop on my laptop just for my business. This way I do not get my business and personal mixed up. So I have a desktop for me, one for business and one for guest.

I also set up all my Word, Excel, etc. documents with the word "mobile," e.g. "mobilesalesdoc."

Also, for folks who live in Washington state & maybe other states, I took a wonderful online business class that was FREE for seven weeks. It was for people with disabilities. They also have a wonderful matching funding program that helps people with disabilities get technical & other equipment.

~ Karen Rosie

Light a Candle, Don't Curse the Darkness

Replacing negative thoughts with positive ones can be transformative for those with ADHD. One of the best examples of positive thinking can be found in the movie Apollo 13. An exploding oxygen tank threatens the spacecraft and the lives of its crew. The astronauts face a horrible dilemma: if they can somehow repair the oxygen system, they still face the very real threat of burning up when the damaged craft re-enters earth's gravity. When the severity of the situation becomes apparent to all, NASA Flight Director, Chris Kraft, and Mission Control commander Gene Kranz have the following exchange:

Chris Kraft: "This could be the worst disaster NASA's ever faced." Gene Kranz: "With all due respect, sir, I believe this is gonna be our finest hour." For me, this quote is a reminder of what positive thinking is really all about.

~Paul O'Connor, MCC

Paul O'Connor coaches business executives with ADHD. He is a Master Certified Coach, secretary of the Professional Association of ADHD Coaches, based in Atlanta. (404) 377-4712 paul@EnergyForLifeCoach.com ~ www.EnergyForLifeCoach.com

Preparing your ODDS and ENDS

Miscellaneous supplies in designated areas help me stay organized and focused. Having these items at my fingertips reduces distractions, saves time, lessens stress, and clears my mind for the bigger tasks. For example:

1. Backyard patio has the basic table, chairs and BBQ grill. In a plastic storage box fitting nicely under the grill are patio tablecloths, ash trays, paper towels, cloth and cleanser, candles, lighter, garbage bags, potholders and grill racks.
2. Front porch consists of chairs and end tables; in a decorative box are lighters, extra candles, ashtray, cloth and cleanser, garbage bags and pen/small notebook.
3. Our laundry room houses all the necessary cleaning supplies for the house. And extra cleansers are in each bathroom under the vanity and under the kitchen sink.
4. Candle lighters are strategically placed in all rooms.
5. Toiletries are in each bathroom and travel-size items are in my desk and car.

~Cindy Giardina, PCC

Cindy Giardina, Professional Certified Coach helping adults and students take charge of their ADHD. cindy@kaleidoscope-coaching.com ~ (973) 694-5077

Be Who You Are

D o you focus on what's wrong about ADHD? Or do you celebrate what's right?

It's your decision. You are a powerful person. You choose in every moment the direction of your life. Take responsibility for who you are and the challenges you face. But never feel ashamed.

Your life is too important. Be who you are. Take a stand for who you are. Your opinion is the only one that matters. Remember that. Life is uncertain and brief. Please do not let doubt diminish the remarkable person that you are. Believe in yourself. Be mindful of whose definition of success you are living by and living with.

For me, success is having the courage and audacity to be exactly who you are. No apologies. Ever. I've never looked at ADHD as a deficit. It's my power. Let it be yours.

~Corinne Rita, CEO

Corinne Rita, CEO of Fierce Focus International, privately trains high octane entrepreneurs and motivates ADHD college students to love who they are. Go to www.findfiercefocus.com to learn more.

Use Your Phone's Navigator as a Time-Management Tool

Your smartphone's navigator is a fine way to get from point A to point B, but did you know it's also a great way to know when to leave?

Let's say you want to arrive someplace by 3:30. Enter your destination in the navigator app and find the "time to destination" feature. If you toggle it (just poke around at it), it can also tell you what time you'd arrive if you were to leave right now.

So if the navigator suggests you'd arrive at 2:45 if you left right now, you know that you can easily hit your 3:30 target. Leave the app running and check in with it over the next 15-30 minutes. The app will update according to changing traffic conditions and recalculate arrival time. As that arrival time approaches 3:30, you know it's time to get moving.

~Dr. Nowell, Ph.D.

Dr. Nowell is a Neuropsychologist offering workshops and clinical services. Contact him at www.DrNowell.com to set up a one-hour ADHD Q & A consultation.

Keep on Bouncing, Rubber!

The first person I knew with ADHD was a kid at summer camp. He was the stereotypical hyperactive kid bouncing off the walls (often literally). He was always getting knocked down, falling, and running into things, and he always bounced back. One day, in a highly competitive camp game, he got slammed face-down into the dirt, hard. Everyone stopped and watched. But he bounced back up ready to play again, earning the nickname "Rubber." That was years ago, long before I knew much about ADHD. Since then, I've often thought of him. I wonder what he's doing and how life has treated him. As adults, getting knocked down in life hurts a lot more and much deeper than hitting the ground face-first on a hot, dry summer day. I hope he kept bouncing back every time life knocked him down, and I hope he's found success and happiness. Keep bouncing, Rubber!

~Rose Smith, M. Ed.

Rose Smith, M. Ed. For more helpful hints and random reflections, please visit http://RandomReflectionsbyRose.wordpress.com/.

Couples & ADHD: Heading Off a Medication Catastrophe

If you take medication for your ADHD, one day you may find yourself somewhere realizing that you have forgotten to bring any medication with you. Head off that crisis by keeping one or two days' worth of medication in your car's glove box. Sounds simple, but here are a few important details that really matter:

1. Always use a pharmacy-labeled bottle

2. Never carry more than a few days' worth in the car

3. Stuff the bottle with tissue to eliminate the rattle

4. Put the pill bottle in an envelope to keep it out of view

5. Remember to refill the bottle when you arrive home

In many states, it is illegal to carry controlled medications without a pharmacy-labeled bottle, and a rattling pill bottle is an open invitation for theft. With these 5 steps, you will be covered legally and emotionally!

~ Sarah A. Ferman, L.M.F.T., P.C.C.
& Robert L. Wilford, Ph.D.

Sarah Ferman, L.M.F.T., P.C.C., & Robert Wilford, Ph.D., are leading ADHD Couples Consultants, helping ADHD Couples reconnect and create loving and enduring relationships. www.ADHDCouplesConsultants.com

Best Time of Day

Do you know what your best time of day is? It is the time of day that you have the most focus and the most energy. In general, it is usually a 2 - 3 hour time period in the day. For some, this time is in the morning, others mid-afternoon. When you decide what your best time of day is, that is the time of day to schedule the things that are hard for you to get started on or just more difficult in general. By scheduling those items in your focus and energy zone, you are more likely to get started and get them done. Identify your best time and then open your calendar and schedule in the hard stuff in those time frames, and you will see you will be more successful in getting the work done.

~Deb Bollom, ADHD & Life Coach

Deb Bollom is a Professional Senior Certified ADHD and Life Coach working with ADHD adults and entrepreneurs who are stuck in details and overwhelm. www.d5coaching.com

ANTS

Ever have thoughts about yourself that are not complimentary or even nice, like "I'm such a dummy," or "I can't do anything right," or "I'll never be a success," or "I'm so stupid"? These types of automatic negative thoughts are called ANTS by Dr. Daniel Amen, author of *Change Your Brain, Change Your Life.* We all have them and think they're "normal." They are learned behavior and they reflect a way we beat ourselves up, repeatedly.

ANTS don't have to be a part of our lives; they can easily be removed! How? It's simple: each time you catch yourself saying something untrue, because these are NOT truths, stop and say a complete opposite statement to yourself, e.g., "I may not understand this, but I'm not dumb," or "I made a mistake and I can fix it," or "I will be successful," or "I am NOT stupid." Try it; it works!

~Dee Shofner Doochin, MLAS, PCC, CMC, PACG, SCAC

Dee Shofner Doochin, MLAS; Professional Certified Coach; Certified Mentor Coach; Senior Certified ADHD Coach; wife, mother, grandmother, and great-grandmother with ADHD; adventurer; lover of life! www.deedoochin.com

A Day at the Movies

Many kids with ADHD have difficulty completing assignments that require them to write a complete story. My own daughter had trouble when she had to write a story about her day. It was hard for her to break the day up and describe the various events. She got overwhelmed and would just write one short sentence that summarized the biggest part of the day. A great exercise to help children compartmentalize things is to ask them to picture their day like it's playing at the movies. Prompt them to use details. What did they see? How did they feel? Have them quickly draw these scenes with stick figures on paper like a storyboard. This helps kids visually break down their day into stages and recall the various events of the day, and it gives them a visual reference to now write a story with a beginning, middle and end.

~Dr. Billi

The AttentionB Method, Pedagogical/Class Management for ADHD with Dr. Billi, Ph.D. Tame the chaos in your classroom using my unique strategies. www.AttentionB.com ~ DrBilli@AttentionB.com ~ (855) DrBilli

How to Reduce Brain Fog and Food Allergies

Do you feel foggy-headed after you eat? Are you bloated or uncomfortable in your intestines? Here's a helpful strategy to address both issues. Your brain affects your intestines and your intestines affect your brain, and they can become part of an endless loop where problems with digestion cause stress for your brain, and problems with your brain cause stress for your digestion.

You'll get the best results when you address both your brain and your intestines. Do brain exercises like the ones that are demonstrated at www.BrainTimeVideos.com and in my other articles found in this book. These exercises strengthen the part of your brain that controls your digestion, and they're key ingredients in your campaign to reduce brain fog and food allergies. To get the best results, do the brain exercises to help your brain AND avoid foods that irritate your intestines to give them time to heal.

~ Dr. Jim Otis, Fellow, American College of Functional Neurology

Dr. Otis specializes in drug-free treatment for ADHD and Learning Disabilities and is the inventor of BrainTime™, a patent-pending technology for optimal brain health. www.BrainTimeVideos.com

Dealing with Anxiety

Many adults with ADHD also suffer from anxiety disorders. Try these techniques to calm and center yourself when anxiety strikes:

1. Leave the location where anxious feelings began. Step outside for a moment, or find a quiet room.

2. Regulate your breathing - 5 seconds in, 5 seconds out - for a period of 3-5 minutes to stabilize your heart rate.

3. Keep a physical object on your person that makes you smile, like a photograph or keychain.

4. Don't rush back into the situation that caused your anxiety.

5. Drink carbonated water to quell nausea.

6. Call someone you trust. You don't have to fight it alone.

7. Do something familiar. For example, memorize a passage from your favorite book and recite it to yourself.

8. Don't feel guilty. Your reactions and feelings are not stupid, ridiculous, or overdramatic. Take a step back, breathe, and try again later.

~Dr. Laurie Senders

Laurie Senders, PhD., Certified Life Coach, and ADHD Coach. Learn more about her coaching at http://www.compellingADHDcoach.com.

Four Natural Ways to Manage Your ADHD

Be **informed:** Each person experiences ADHD differently, and the only way to really understand your ADHD, and how best to manage it, is to learn as much about ADHD as possible.

Be well rested: Getting enough sleep is truly one of the best ways you can minimize your ADHD symptoms. I have seen huge improvement in people's ADHD symptoms simply by getting adequate, consistent sleep.

Enjoy your sense of humor: Being able to laugh at yourself, and the inevitable "ADD" things you do, is a great coping strategy. Maintaining a sense of humor allows us to forgive ourselves and prevents that annoying negative thinking.

Cherish good friends: Having people around who love you and your ADHD is one of the best "natural ways" to manage your ADHD. Supportive family or friends that "get" you is crucial to feeling satisfied in our lives.

~Laurie Dupar, PMHNP, RN, ADHD Coach

Laurie Dupar is a trained psychiatric nurse practitioner and Certified ADHD Coach. You can find out more about working with her at (917) 791-1799 or www.coachingforadhd.com.

Natural Abilities

Someone told our group to "think outside the box." A lone voice answered, "Why does there have to be a box?" In the thoughtful silence that followed, you could practically hear the heartbeats of everyone in the room. Seeing the whole world instead of just a box is much better. You will be able to visualize what career paths will work for you. When you embrace your own natural abilities and hidden strengths, you will finally be capable of tailoring a plan of action. And you will be pleasantly surprised with the results!

~Dulce Torres, LPC-S, BCC, ADHD Coach

Dulce Torres, Licensed Professional Counselor/Supervisor, Board Certified Coach, specializes in ADHD coaching that helps teenagers, adults, and parents to find their hidden strengths. www.dstcoaching.com ~ dtorres@dstcoaching.com

Continue Dating Your Mate!

Keep dating your spouse after marriage, babies, or career changes. Make it a weekly habit. It can be just an hour and not cost money; however, it must be quality time together. Turn *off* the electronic devices and leave distractions behind; yes, that means no texting or cell phones! Have fun, laugh, hold hands, alternate which spouse chooses the venue or activity, try new interests/classes or revive memories from pre-marriage days. *The 7 Habits of Highly Effective People* author Stephen Covey advised: "Put deposits in the emotional bank account often, so there is something to draw from on a bad day." ADHDers usually have many moments when ADHD shows up and adversely affects the relationship. Good to have some "money in the bank" for those times! Remember to focus on activities that give you a positive experience and time to connect and refresh.

~Sherry Clarke, MA, LCMFT, ACG

Sherry Clarke, MA, LCMFT, a veteran Licensed Marriage and Family Therapist and ADHD Coach, has a passion for helping couples and parents understand, embrace and celebrate their ADHD. www.clarkecoaching.com

Pause for Fine Tuning

Irrational, impulsive ideas can create communication troubles. My daughter, 23, who was diagnosed with ADHD in 2010, is a very impulsive girl. Her academic life is highly affected by impulsivity. She misses her classes on impulse, choosing to do something else, which leads to tension between us. Knowing about ADHD, I learned to approach her differently. For example, when she calls me with an irrational, impulsive wish, I buy time by asking her to talk about it later that day. By the time we get to talk, she usually drops the idea of doing it. When I ask her to talk about it, she tells me that she is not really available to make it happen at that time. An unexpected, irrational wish can be defeated if you allow the person time to pause before you attack him/her. Pausing is vital in order to build fulfilling communications with your loved ones.

~Eda Aydogan, MA, ACC, PACG

Eda Aydogan, MA, ACC, PACG, ADHD Coach, specializes in helping you understand your own ADHD and find coping strategies. For more information, find me at http://www.dehbka.com. eaydogan@dehbka.com

Sometimes You Have to Use Logic

The kitchen's a mess, the counters cluttered, dirty dishes all over the place. Ugh, cleaning. I'm overwhelmed, my brain skittering around, trying to hide. I recognize this situation. There is something I can do, but I don't **feel** like doing **anything**. Recognize **that** situation too. The answer? Unpalatable. Use logic.

Logic says: 1) it won't take long; 2) it won't be that unpleasant; 3) you will feel **much** better afterwards; and 4) between now and starting you will kick and scream like a grouchy toddler, but that doesn't negate the truth of points 1 to 3. So, big breath OUT. And start. And, of course, before long, it's finished.

We ADHDers absolutely hate doing really, really trivial things. Boring, to us, makes us want to twist and squirm and do absolutely anything else. No, not washing the dishes! The worst thing on earth! It's not. Sometimes you have to use logic.

~Dr. Gillian Hayes, Ph.D.

Gillian Hayes, PhD, is an ADHD coach who specializes in helping students, academics and other high achievers dig out their best. gillian@brightshinycoaching.com

Five Tips to Improve Your Child's Behavior

Parents of ADHD children can feel frustration with their child's impulsivity, inattention and restlessness. Try these tips to help children control their behavior and still maintain their natural curiosity and enthusiasm:

1. Be clear with the rules in advance. Briefly and calmly remind your child what is expected of them.

2. Answer the "why." Children with ADHD often comprehend things concretely and benefit from a simple statement as to "why."

3. Establish consequences. By sharing upfront what will happened if they misbehave, discipline becomes more matter of fact.

4. Develop a "signal." A signal can alert kids if they're starting to misbehave and help them stay on track.

5. Foster consistency. ADHD children are naturally inconsistent. As parents, we become the model for consistency through our follow-through.

~Laurie Dupar, PMHNP, RN, PCC, Certified ADHD Coach and Nurse Practitioner

Laurie Dupar is a Certified ADHD Coach and trained psychiatric nurse practitioner who has specialized in ADHD for the past nine years. www.coachingforadhd.com

Hire a Coach to Help You Help Your Kid

The simple truth about childhood ADHD: ADHD is an ongoing issue requiring management, and kids need help from parents to learn to manage their ADHD.

The simple truth about parents of kids with ADHD: Parents need support & guidance to help their kids most effectively; parent training provides the tools parents need for ADHD management; and coaching helps parents make the training stick, teaching them to turn information into action and offering an accountability structure.

The obvious solution: Parents are the missing link in ADHD treatment. Parents, when you get the help you need, your confidence increases, you meet the needs of your ADHD kids, and you rediscover the joy of family life. You are your child's secret weapon. Pay attention to yourself. Take care of yourself. And invest in a coach for yourself.

~ Elaine Taylor-Klaus, CPCC, ACC, and Diane Dempster, MHSA, CPC, ACC

ImpactADHD helps parents help kids. Elaine Taylor-Klaus & Diane Dempster provide reality-based training, with coaching to make it stick. We help your family thrive! http://www.ImpactADHD.com

"The secret to success is learning to go from failure to failure without loss of enthusiasm."

~ Winston Churchill

"YES!" Days

Wouldn't it be nice to have an entire day where you were told "YES!"? Children and adults alike may feel overwhelmed by directions, negativity, and a lack of control by being told *no* they *can't* all day. My family came up with "YES! days." One full day from breakfast to bedtime they get, within reason, to hear the most agreeable, pleasant word in the English language! They pick the agenda for the day (you give them examples to choose from and they can add their requests as well). For example, if they want ice cream for dinner, your answer would be, "Yes! We can have ice cream after dinner tonight!

Or, if it has been a particularly great day, we would say "yes!" to having ice cream for dinner! We just get creative with our answers. It's a way for the ADDer to fill up their love tank with a positive day!

~Erica Kress, M.S.W., ADHD Life Coach

Erica Kress is a Social Worker and Life Coach who specializes in helping adults and children not only to manage their symptoms of AD/HD, but to THRIVE!

Make Your Own Coaching Tips List

We already know many of our weaknesses and strengths. Let's use them! Make your list:

• **What are your strengths?** Certain subjects, like Math or English? Certain sports or games like aerobic sports or board games like chess? Accounting, sales, or production?

• **When are you most efficient?** Early morning or late afternoon? After aerobic exercise? Before a good meal you look forward to, or after?

• **Where do you work or study best?** In the library? Your room? At a coffee shop? In a vacant lab? In an empty conference room?

• **In what situations do you make friends best?** Small groups? Big meetings, like conferences? Party atmosphere?

Then plan your life to take advantage of those strengths and avoid those weaknesses!

~ Hervé J. LeBoeuf, III, Ph.D.

Dr. LeBoeuf, Life and ADHD Coach, leads people with ADHD, of all ages and worldwide, to success by working with their unique brains. HLeBoeuf@Gmail.com ~ (703) 455-4144

Age is Not a Disease

I learned I had ADD when I was 75. It was a relief, because I thought there was something much more seriously wrong with me. Now that I know more about the disorder, I am delighted to have ADD. ADD is inherited; our children and grandchildren may have it, and there is no shame in that. When understood and treated, it is an asset! It is not only a childhood disorder but accompanies us throughout our lives. Young adults with ADD may have parents or grandparents who are suffering now. Offer them hope.

The 60+ ADD group is the most neglected group of sufferers. Some health professionals ignore the ADD possibility and attribute the symptoms to something else, sometimes suggesting their age is to blame. Never accept that reason. A wise doctor once told me, "age is not a disease." Please seek help for elder ADDers in your life.

~Jane Patrick, BA, MEd.

Jane Patrick, retired teacher, diagnosed with ADD at age 75. Enjoying the trip! Advocate for neglected group of 60+ ADDers. janeham@abacom.com

Walk a Mile in Another's Shoes

This is an exercise that I use with couples, parents and children, co-workers, or between anyone who cannot see the other party's standpoint. I ask them to play role reversal. They take turns speaking to each other from the point-of-view of the other person. I ask them to use a symbol, like a piece of clothing or hat, that will make them feel like they're really in the other party's shoes. The rules are strictly this: be as present as possible and really hear your partner. It's okay if an occasional time-out is needed to cool down. The purpose is to understand how your partner feels in the relationship from his/her perspective rather than your own. This psychodrama exercise is great because it uses all of your senses, bypasses your cognition and goes to a more emotional, deeper level of understanding each other.

~Dr. Billi

The AttentionB Method, Pedagogical/Class Management for ADHD with Dr. Billi, Ph.D. Tame the chaos in your classroom using my unique strategies. www.AttentionB.com ~ DrBilli@AttentionB.com ~ (855) DrBilli

Breadcrumbs for Productivity?

Transitions and getting started with tasks can be challenging for people with ADHD. One of the most difficult transitions can be the transition between ending one work day and beginning the next. The idea of leaving breadcrumbs can help on both sides of the transition. The idea of breadcrumbs comes from the fairytale Hansel and Gretel where Hansel left a trail of breadcrumbs to follow.

Breadcrumbs, for us, take the form of leaving information about where we are in a task so that we can pick up there the next day. At the end of the day, take an index card and write down information about where you are in a task or project. This helps with the transitioning away part. Then write down the steps that you want to begin with the next day. Review it when you arrive at work for a quick start to the next day.

~Jay Carter, MBA, ACG

Jay Carter is an adult ADHD coach specializing in personal productivity and workplace issues. Learn more about Jay's practice at www.hyperfocusedcoaching.com or jaycarter@hyperfocusedcoaching.com.

How to Help My Grandchild with ADHD

If you are a grandparent who suspects your grandchild has ADHD but your family is not ready to look at the possibility of the diagnosis, here are a few suggestions:

Maintain a neutral, supportive presence. Staying neutral now increases the chances you'll be listened to when the opportunity arises at a later date.

Give them time. Know each family/parent needs to take their own steps in their own time to find out more about ADHD and what it will mean to their family.

Find your own support. Finally, consider working with an ADHD coach. A coach can help you sort through your own frustrations and introduce strategies that can support your grandchild in small ways.

By positioning yourself as an encouraging member of the family with pure intentions, you leave the door open to a future where your grandchild is surrounded with love.

~Laurie Dupar, PMHNP, RN, PCC Certified ADHD Coach and Nurse Practitioner

Laurie Dupar, a trained psychiatric nurse practitioner, coach and author, is an internationally-recognized expert on ADHD. Contact her at (916) 791-1799 or www.coachingforadhd.com.

Living in a Non-ADD World

Metaphorically, having ADHD is like being born left-handed in a right-handed world. Society and the self-help section in bookstores are quick to suggest a right-handed solution. The ah-ha comes when those with ADHD realize (and attend to) the fact that they are essentially born left-handed (and have different brain wiring). When they do, solutions become more obvious: If you're left-handed and play golf, use a left-handed set of golf clubs. Notice, metaphorically, the person didn't change; he was always left-handed, but his behavior changed when he attended to being left-handed. Attend to being ADHD and you'll find ADHD solutions!

~Jeff Copper, MBA, PCC, ACG, CPCC

Jeff Copper, MBA, PCC, ACG, CPCC, is an attention coach, founder of DIG Coaching Practice, and host of Attention Talk Radio...Your ADHD Information Station! www.digcoaching.com

Winding Down Between Your Worlds

Many of us dwell in various worlds throughout the day. For example, some of us might go from the *parent* world in the morning to the *professional* world at work to the *spouse* world at home to the *friend* world on weekends. Going from world to world can be bumpy sometimes. We tend to carry over residual feelings (like a hard day at the office or a hectic morning with the kids) from one world to the other. To avoid this, allow yourself some time to unwind in between your worlds. On the way home from work, put on music for a few minutes that changes your frame of mind, relaxes or energizes you before you get home. Or before going to work, take a few minutes of time to yourself. Allow your mind and body to shift from one world to the other as you breathe and exhale.

~Dr. Billi

The AttentionB Method, Pedagogical/Class Management for ADHD with Dr. Billi, Ph.D. Tame the chaos in your classroom using my unique strategies. www.AttentionB.com ~ DrBilli@AttentionB.com ~ (855) DrBilli

Time for Dessert!

It's Saturday night. The family is out for dinner, but the kids are fighting. You've threatened no dessert, again. You really don't want to do it, because the evening will be ruined. But your patience is about gone. You reach across the table and take five sugar packets from the holder. You put them in the middle of the table.

"Listen. Every time mom or I have to tell you to cool it, you lose one. If any are left when dinner's over, we'll have dessert. No sugar packets, no dessert." Are the kids impressed? No; they have another loud argument. Without saying anything, you reach across and remove a packet.

Two more times, you need to take away packets. But then they see that only two are left. They seem to realize that they might not have dessert. It's quiet. They are playing a game, entertaining themselves.

Time for dessert!

~ Jeffrey S. Katz, Ph.D., Clinical Psychologist

Dr. Jeffrey Katz, clinical psychologist, expert in the evaluation and treatment of AD/HD, learning and behavior problems. Helping individuals and families to succeed. www.DrJeffreyKatz.com

The Internal Pause Button

Impulse control is one of the things that cause the most issues for my ADHD clients. While the intention isn't always malicious, the final result becomes the issue. I advise my clients to invent an "internal pause button." This is a two-step process. The first step asks two questions: "what is my intention?" and "what is the intended result?" Once you've successfully answered the first two questions, the second step ties the first two questions together by asking, "is this worth the potential consequence(s)?" For example, if you're unhappy at work and you want to explain your issue(s) to your boss, you may find good answers to the first step but realize that you may lose your job, which isn't a good result or second step. This strategy takes time and effort, but with practice, you will find yourself making less impulsive decisions and beginning to see better results.

~Jonathan D. Carroll, M.A.

Jonathan D. Carroll is considered an expert on ADHD and works as a coach in the Chicagoland area. Please visit http://www.adhdcoachchicago.com for more information.

Responding to Emails

Situation: I have to answer my emails but there's too many. It's no surprise that communications have changed, especially with emails. The email comes in and we read it and then all too often, we say to ourselves "I'll answer it later." But we forget, later never comes, and the sender is left wondering if you got the message.

Consider this: When someone is standing in front of you and asks a question, you give a response; you don't just stare at them. When you're on the phone and someone tells you something, you give a response, not dead air time. Why shouldn't emails be the same? Save the embarrassment of having to make an excuse for not getting back with someone, even if it's only to respond by saying, "got your message," "thank you," or "call you later."

~Joyce Kubik, ADHD Coach, CC (IAC)

Joyce Kubik, Certified Life and ADHD Coach for students and adults, author of planning journals developed specifically for ADHD. Find it and more at www.bridgetosuccess.net.

Neon Bright

If your office desk is, like mine, filled with papers from a variety of projects and ideas, it can be almost impossible at times to find one particular piece among the piles. Although I am fairly organized, there are days when my enthusiasm doesn't leave time for me to put everything in its place.

One solution that I found works amazingly well is copying the information that I know I will use over and over again, such as email addresses, phone numbers and even my daily planner sheet onto brightly-colored neon paper. That way, when I'm searching my desk for my daily planner, the bright blue/yellow/green paper jumps out at me like a neon sign from among a stack of white papers! Using the same color for the same information makes it easier to find and saves me oodles of time and frustration!

~Laurie Dupar, PMHNP, RN, PCC, Certified ADHD Coach and Nurse Practitioner

Laurie Dupar, Senior Certified ADHD Coach, is an internationally-known expert on ADHD. You can reach her at (916) 791-1799 or www.coachingforadhd.com.

Do-Overs

When we react out of frustration, it is important to admit our mistake, apologize, and start again; our children should be taught to do the same. Second chances are critical to a harmonious family. I call these moments "Do Overs." Research shows that negative feedback does not teach. When you find yourself in a situation where you react inappropriately and your child begins to argue back, call out "Do Over." Then walk away until the two of you calm down. When you return, show your vulnerability by admitting your mistake, apologize, and begin again. This is an important teaching moment.

All members of the family should have the same rights. Mistakes are an important part of life. Do Overs immediately diffuse a negative situation. Everyone knows they will be allowed to take back their actions and words and be given a second chance to do or say things differently.

~Judith Champion, MSW, ACG

Judith Champion, MSW, ACG, ADHD Family Coach and Educator. ADHD affects the whole family. Coaching for parents, children and adults.   www.ADHDAssociates.com   ~   (609)   468-0819 judith@judithchampion.com

Fix It? Really?

I like to call my generation (30-45 years), the fix-it generation. We are driven into action almost unconsciously when a person, process, system or thing does not act, look, sound, achieve, or feel the way we want it to, and we all know that the road less travelled is overrated. So, we are the busiest people ever to grace this planet. As our knowledge and toys advanced, our human interaction and essence diminished proportionately. No wonder we find it a frustrating challenge, having to cater to clients and children and loved ones and work colleagues that just don't get it and, even worse, don't want to get it! They want the one thing we don't have enough of: our time and undivided attention. No multi-tasking allowed when you are with them. So, we do what we do best: try and fix it. Really?

~Juliet Victor, Performance Coach

Juliet Victor, Certified Performance Coach specializing in transformation and behavioral coaching, and aspiring Consciousness Coach. Juliet.victor@vodamail.co.za

Parking Made Easy

The best invention for the distracted, disorganized shopper? The car locking beep! I never seem to remember where I park my car, sometimes not even the general area! I've been known to wander the lot, swearing the car was in that row, but later finding I was completely off (and yes, I avoid multilevel garages as much as possible).

Then I purchased a car with a keyless entry system that beeps if I press the automatic lock button twice. No more wandering...no more embarrassment that I can't find the car. I can simply press the button and listen for the beep to lead me to where I need to go!

~Meg Gehan, LCSW

Meg Gehan, LCSW, is the owner of Outside the Box Marketing, where she helps her clients find more time to do the work they love. http://outsidetheboxmarking.org

Battling Boredom in the Classroom

My fifteen-year-old client and I assessed one of his impairments of ADHD that has contributed significant struggles to sustaining focus in class. The boredom he feels is physiological, but he only knows that he has had trouble overcoming this feeling and as a result misses information. He told me one day that he often has many Internet browsers open on his laptop during classes. When he becomes bored and can't focus, he switches to a browser covering a topic of interest, like the stock market or flight patterns. After a few minutes, depending on the degree of boredom, he switches back to the topic at hand, renewed and able to focus! He never read anything about the meaning behind what he did. What he did out of desperation allowed him to re-fuel and independently transition back to class, successfully completing the goal without class disruption and negative attention.

~Karen K. Lowry, R.N., M.S.N., ADHD Coach, AAC

Karen K. Lowry is an ADHD Coach who specializes in supporting children and teens to formulate goals and develop action plans to achieve success! www.addadvocate.com

Your Powerful ADHD Brain is Different. Don't Try to Make it Work Like Other Brains!

Your brain is unique to you! You have special gifts and abilities that others will never know! Others may tell you how their brains work and think yours should work the same as theirs. Listen to your own brain. Pay heed to tips in this book, use your own techniques you have developed, or listen to someone who understands your ADHD brain. Write lists, break big tasks into smaller tasks, use a detailed calendar, check your work often, and give yourself small rewards for work well done. You can be as successful as you want!

~ Hervé J. LeBoeuf, III, Ph.D.

Dr. LeBoeuf, Life and ADHD Coach, leads people with ADHD, of all ages and worldwide, to success by working with their unique brains. HLeBoeuf@Gmail.com ~ (703) 455-4144

Rules Really Do Make the Game

People with ADD often balk at rules and structures. However, rules and structures are actually what help us to enjoy whatever game we play.

Let's look at American football. Rules govern the number of: players on the field, yards in a down, downs per possession and seconds on the clock. The lines on the field (providing boundaries and structures) guide the players and spectators in how the team is progressing. These same markings help the athletes judge what is needed to reach their goal.

If you take away the structure of the rules and boundaries of the field markings, you take away the sport. Neither the athletes nor the fans understand how to play the game. In fact, the game no longer exists. Compare your life or business to a sport you love. What are your rules and boundaries? How do they guide you? How do you know when you have scored?

~Kricket Harrison, CPCC, ACC, PACG,
Professional Coach & Speaker

Kricket Harrison, Professional Coach and very passionate amateur tennis player, helps students, athletes and professionals SCORE on the field and in life. www.BrightOutsidetheBox.com

"The secret to success is consistency of purpose."

~ Benjamin Disraeli

A Plan for Planning

Just as a business needs a strategic plan to move forward and grow, so do you! To start, make a list of everything you want to do, whether it be right now, in six months or five years from now. Just throw all your ideas on paper, no judgments.

Walk away from the list. Let it percolate. Then come back and sort the ideas into three lists: "Right now," "In the near future," and "Way down the road."

Walk away from the lists. Let them percolate. Then come back and play. Put the ideas for each list into the order that makes sense to you; it maybe importance, timeframe or some other measure. Try different ways until you find the mix that makes the most sense to you.

Walk away. Let it percolate.

Come back and make any adjustments you feel necessary. Now you have a plan!

~Abigail Wurf, M.Ed., CLC

Abigail Wurf, M.Ed., CLC, coaches executives, entrepreneurs, couples and other adults affected by ADHD. Serving Washington DC and nationally. awurf@verizon.net ~ abigailwurf.com ~ (202) 244-2234

4 Strategies for Using Timers

Here are great ways to use timers:
1) Leave On Time With Two Timers: Set the first timer for 10 minutes before you need to leave to give yourself transition time. Set the second timer for 2 minutes before you need to leave so you know when to walk out the door.

2) Race the Clock: When you procrastinate about household chores, play "race the clock." For example, set the timer for 15 minutes and straighten the kitchen. Work as fast as you can and stop when the timer sounds.

3) Get Started: It can be difficult to start a big project. Next time you are stuck on how to start, set a timer for 15 minutes and do ANYTHING related to the project.

4) Analog vs. Digital: Whenever possible, use an analog-type timer like the Time Timer® so you can visualize time passing.

~Laura Rolands, ADHD Coach

Laura Rolands is an ADHD Coach who helps clients manage time, reduce interruptions, focus on priorities, increase productivity and achieve goals. Learn more at www.MyAttentionCoach.com.

How is ADHD Diagnosed?

ADHD is diagnosed through a process of assessment interviews in which your history and how your everyday experiences (at home, school or work) are noted. The three key areas that are focused on with a possible ADHD diagnosis are challenges with attention, hyperactivity or impulsivity. ADHD is a diagnosis of "exclusion." This means that the questions asked will help to eliminate other causes. Before making a diagnosis, a thorough medical examination needs to have been done to rule out physical causes of ADHD symptoms. The diagnosis needs to be made by a professional with training in ADHD such as psychiatrists, nurse practitioners, psychologists, neurologists, and clinical social workers. To make a diagnosis of ADHD, professionals use a list taken directly from the *Diagnostic and Statistical Manual of Mental Disorders.* Your answers, experiences, behaviors, symptoms, etc., are what helps to determine if it is ADHD or perhaps something else.

~Laurie Dupar, PMHNP, RN, PCC, Certified ADHD Coach and Nurse Practitioner

Laurie Dupar, PMHNP, RN, PCC, is a trained psychiatric mental health nurse practitioner and certified ADHD coach. You can find out more at www.coachingforadhd.com.

Getting U.N.S.T.U.C.K.

Do you ever find yourself spending hours on a task only to realize you haven't made any progress? Being stuck can be frustrating, disheartening, and overwhelming. This happens to all of us, and there are ways to break through the cycle.

One such method is to get yourself U.N.S.T.U.C.K.:

Use New Strategies To Untangle Cognitive Kinks

Changing your thinking can make it easier to change your actions. Often, after employing this simply tweak, you'll find you have more energy and focus and you'll no longer be stuck!

~Laurie Moore Skillings, SCAC

Laurie Moore Skillings is a Senior Certified ADHD Coach who uses a unique combination of advising and advocacy to help students thrive academically. www.addwithease.com

Asking for Help Brings Empowerment

Everyone needs help sometimes. While many may consider asking for help as a sign of weakness, in actuality it's a major strength. Knowing yourself, recognizing and admitting when you have problems and taking the initiative to solve them is a huge step toward a more relaxed, confident you! Find someone you trust and respect. Someone you've had successful, positive interactions with in the past. This person could be a friend, coworker, relative or even a coach. If someone puts you down, don't approach them again for help. Nothing says you have only one go-to person.

You should never feel ashamed or guilty asking for help or advice. You are not defined by your ADHD, but you do have to learn how to manage it so it doesn't hinder your ability to be productive. Having a support structure is a powerful tool in achieving your dreams!

~Dr. Laurie Senders, Ph.D.

Dr. Laurie Senders, Certified Life Coach, and ADHD Coach transforms women entrepreneurs into organized, time-oriented, money-producing people. drlsenders@comcast.net

The 7-Step PowerPlan to Success™ with ADHD

Creating positive change is a difficult process for anyone but can be even more complicated when ADHD gets in the way. The 7-Step PowerPlan to Success™ with ADHD is a blueprint of specific steps designed to help you clarify and accomplish goals. It is my paradigm for self-coaching. Our ability to successfully strategize and take action is dependent on understanding, and working with, the way we think. For most people with ADHD, the "Just Do It" phrase popularized by Nike is not often an option. If we could, we would. Working with your unique strengths *and* challenges, learn how to get out of your own way and get things done.

Take the next seven days to explore these PowerPlan to Success™ Steps one at a time. Begin with WHO you are and move on to WHAT you want. You'll find that it IS possible to transform the way you think, work and live!

~Susan Lasky, MA, BCC, SCAC

Susan Lasky, Master ADD/ADHD Strategist, Productivity Coach & Professional Organizer, creator of the 7-Step PowerPlan to Success™ and the 28-Day Accountability Challenge™. www.SusanLasky.com ~ www.PowerPlanToSuccess.com ~ Susan@SusanLasky.com

Have You Reached a "Tipping Point"?

A "tipping point" is a time in people's lives when the strategies they have been using to manage their ADHD challenges no longer seem to be working. It is often experienced along with feelings of overwhelm and chaos. In fact, life might seem to be falling apart in a big way. Prior to a tipping point, you might not have even known that ADHD existed. Normal life changes can bring on a tipping point and might include:

- School changes
- Transitioning into a new role at work
- Physical injury
- Moving
- Changes in family dynamics

Reaching your tipping point is beyond your control and doesn't mean you have failed; rather, it means that you are at a crossroads. By learning new ways to cope, you can get your life/career/family back on track!

~Laurie Dupar, PMHNP, RN, ADHD Coach

To find out more about tipping points and what you can do, go to www.coachingforadhd.com or call Laurie at (916) 791-1799.

Nine Practical Steps That Could Save Your Job

You just missed another deadline. You've tried every possible treatment for your ADHD, but now it's too late. How can you save your job?

1. Be honest with yourself; claim the problems you caused.

2. Write down all your positive efforts (including ADHD treatment).

3. Mentally switch places with your boss; what is his or her real objective?

4. Call on your true Authentic Self to evaluate whether you can meet those expectations.

5. Make the first move; set an appointment with your boss.

6. Don't complain or ask for special treatment.

7. Take responsibility without groveling or getting emotional.

8. Offer practical, immediate solutions to previous problems.

9. Know that whatever happens, you will survive.

~Linda Roggli, PCC

Linda Roggli, PCC; award-winning author of *Confessions of an ADDiva - Midlife in the Non-Linear Lane* and ADHD coach/retreat facilitator, supporting women 40-and-better at www.addiva.net.

A Nonverbal Connection with Others

This is a fun and creative exercise that coaches, parents or teachers can use to teach clients, couples or students about the boundaries and flexibility of relationships. You'll need a roll of crepe paper. The instructor can decide how much length should be used according to age, relationship, symptoms, behavior, etc. Have two people each hold one end of the paper. They must dance whenever music comes on and freeze whenever it stops, making their way around the room. They cannot use vocal language. They must only use nonverbal communication, so they really have to focus on each other's expressions, read their body language and tune into their needs. The paper is delicate, like relationships, and certain moves will cause it to rip. They can tie it back together if needed and start over. The goal is to teach them metaphorically about the importance of communication in their relationships.

~Dr. Billi

The AttentionB Method, Pedagogical/Class Management for ADHD with Dr. Billi, Ph.D. Tame the chaos in your classroom using my unique strategies. www.AttentionB.com ~ DrBilli@AttentionB.com ~ (855) DrBilli

Top 10 Ways to Love Your Partner: Even if They Don't Have ADHD

Here are ten ways to show your love:

1. Tell them what you love about them.

2. Put your mobile device down and step away from the computer when communicating with them.

3. Ask them what they need. Be sure to listen to the answer!

4. Laugh with them. If you are not feeling funny, look for a joke online.

5. Put important dates on the calendar.

6. Be specific about what you need from them and tell them how it will help you.

7. Do not judge.

8. Know the impact you have on them.

9. Make time to do something special for them.

10. Educate them about ADHD in small chunks. Give them time to absorb information.

~Lisa Boester, ADHD Coach

Lisa Boester is a professionally-trained ADHD Coach and Consultant. From business owners to homemakers, she has a diverse client family.   lbboester@gmail.com   ~   (317)   879-6457 www.adhdartoflife.com

Monkeys in a Tree

I once learned meditation from a guru who said, "Our thoughts are jabbering monkeys in a tree." He also said that meditation could quiet the monkeys, and this was true, if I continued to be faithful to the practice of meditation. "The first 20 years would be the most difficult," he said. My loyalty to meditation was flawed, and my monkeys won out in the long run.

After being diagnosed with ADD recently, meditation was suggested. I went back to quieting my monkeys and have found some peace and serenity in meditation the way I was taught years ago. It calms my thoughts, lowers my heartbeat and blood pressure, and when done in the morning, makes my day run more smoothly. It costs nothing and can be done in any quiet place. Meditation is medication for ADD. My monkeys are subdued.

~Jane Patrick, BA, MEd.

Jane Patrick, retired teacher, diagnosed with ADD at age 75. Now enjoying the trip! Advocate for neglected group of 60+ ADDers. janeham@abacom.com

What Accommodations Should Be Added to An IEP or 504 Plan?

Many ADHD children have an IEP or 504 accommodation plan; however, selecting accommodations for the classroom is often ignored. Parents must add effective strategies and ensure ALL teachers follow them. Accommodations to consider:

1. Extra time for assignments, homework and tests.
2. Separate location for tests.
3. Preferential seating.
4. Extra textbooks for home use.
5. Writing assignments done on the computer or iPad.
6. Directions repeated and explained several times.
7. Frequent breaks, with child able to request breaks.
8. Student is allowed to doodle or engage in other "fidgets."
9. Use of large pencils or other adaptations to classroom tools.
10. Use of a tape recorder.
11. Modified homework.
12. Creation of a reward system.
13. Given a hard copy of all lectures.
14. Cues and prompts to stay on task.
15. Instruction and tests given in smaller "chunks."

~Lisa-Anne Ray-Byers, MS-CCC-SLP, MS-Ed, SDA

Lisa-Anne Ray-Byers is a speech-language pathologist, author and columnist specializing in pediatric speech and language disorders. www.AskLisaAnne.com.

TriADD Mates: A Tribute to ADDCA Learning Groups

The three of us met as randomly assigned learning partners at the ADD Coach Academy. We all have learning challenges connected to our individual AD/HD, and no one expected much from our impending group experience. Calling from Canada and the USA, we met online to share coursework, and, eventually our lives. We talked about daily successes and challenges, clarified new information, had the occasional rant, and always inspired and energized each other. We created a safe space, and when those key AD/HD characteristics of impulsivity, distractibility and hyperactivity showed up, they were never judged but understood for what they were. A sense of belonging allowed each of us to be who we are, with no apology or pretense. We found the experience of acceptance within a group of peers empowering. The synergy we create by connection is real and tangible; it pulls us forward. We want this experience for you.

~Lynne Biddle-Walker, Dr. David E. Klein, and Monika Pompetzki, ADHD Coaches

Lynne Biddle-Walker: (615) 442-1049 ~ Lynnebw@gmail.com
Dr. David E. Klein: (516) 621-4030 ~ drdekleindpm@verizon.net
Monika Pompetzki: (905) 336-8330 ~ monika@add-adhdCoaching.com

The Language of Us and We

I use the following exercise for couples who constantly point the finger at each other. Because the language of "you" and "I" can come across as accusatory or as if you're singling the other person out, I ask them to shift to the language of "us" and "we." This forces them to consider both of their needs when they are speaking to each other. They must work together as equals in this language. For example, instead of one partner saying to the other, "You are working too many hours," they can reframe it by saying, "We don't spend enough time together because of work." It totally changes the meaning and puts the onus on both of them to discuss it and find a solution together. More importantly, it takes the blame out of the equation. This exercise is not just limited to couples. It can also be beneficial between siblings, parents and children, teachers and students.

~Dr. Billi

The AttentionB Method, Pedagogical/Class Management for ADHD with Dr. Billi, Ph.D. Tame the chaos in your classroom using my unique strategies. www.AttentionB.com ~ DrBilli@AttentionB.com ~ (855) DrBilli

Calm Down, Don't Melt Down

We all have moments where we feel out of control or ticked-off. With a little thought and planning, we can reduce the escalation and regain our sense of balance. Here are two brain-based strategies to keep your calm when the sparks are flying:

1. **Breathe slowly.** Simple, but it really works. Why? Because when your frontal lobes are fueled with oxygen, they function better. So, sit down, close your eyes and breathe three deep, slow breaths in and out.

2. **Walk backwards** with one foot directly behind the other. When you walk backward, you engage the cerebellum, which shifts the focus of your mental energy away from frustration, anger and pain and into concentrated movement. That motor-to-cognition connection is the magic missing piece in our work with ADHD. Get moving to calm down.

~Lynne Kenney, Psy.D.

Lynne Kenney, Psy.D., is a mother of two, a practicing pediatric psychologist in Scottsdale, AZ, and the creator of The Family Coach Method. Her NEW co-authored book, *Time-In not Time-Out,* is available this Fall on Kindle. For more visit www.lynnekenney.com.

What's Your Disco Ball?

People with ADHD are attracted to things that are different. This has been called the "Shiny Object Syndrome," or the tendency to be easily distracted by something new or unique. We are told to ignore these shiny things and stick to the plan. Mostly, this doesn't work, because noticing new things is an ADHD strength. It's what makes us great problem-solvers, inventors and creators.

Instead of ignoring them, realize that you are going to notice shiny things, but in order to accomplish goals and stay motivated, learn what _your_ shiniest, brightest object, a.k.a. "disco ball," is. Ask yourself, "What is it that outshines the rest?" Is it your family, money, your health? Write it down. Get a picture of it. Say it out loud.

The next time you notice those pesky shiny objects and are feeling unfocused, remember your "disco ball" to keep you on the right track.

~Laurie Dupar, PMHNP, RN, PCC Certified ADHD Coach and Nurse Practitioner

Laurie Dupar is a senior certified ADHD coach, author and speaker. (916) 791-1799 ~ www.coachingforadhd.com

Meditation Made Easy

Meditation is highly recommended for ADHD, with benefits such as mental clarity and increased attention, memory, and well-being. To calm your mind, open your heart! And try one of these:

-Stare at a candle flame.

-Find and use a special "me-time cushion."

-Create a mantra and repeat it 100 times.

-Study your arms slowly. Starting from one shoulder, move down towards your hand, then to the other hand and up the other arm.

-Focus on your breath. Imagine a colorful light flowing through your body from head to toe to earth.

-On a hard surface, trace a spiral with your finger forwards and backwards, repeatedly.

Do 3-minute sessions. Build to 15 minutes max. Use a timer. Sit or walk as it fits.

~Melissa Fahrney, M.A., CPC

Melissa Fahrney, certified ADHD Coach, School Psychologist, Meditation Instructor, HeartMath™ Provider, Mom and ADDer extraordinaire, helps young people strategize and succeed using heart intelligence. www.facebook.com/addheartworks.

"It is not enough to be busy. So are the ants. The question is: What are we busy about?"

~ Henry David Thoreau

Hungry for Frog?

"If the first thing you do when you wake up is eat a live frog, then nothing worse can happen for the rest of the day!" Brian Tracy, authority on the development of human potential, says your "frog" should be the most difficult item on your to-do list, the one you're most likely to procrastinate on. If you eat that first, it'll give you energy and momentum for the rest of the day. Letting your "frog" sit and stare at you while you do unimportant things drains your energy and occupies brain space without you even realizing it. Ask yourself:

- What's your frog?
- What will you gain by eating that frog?
- How can you take the first bite or step?
- What will be easier after you eat it?
- Take 5 minutes for exercise, then sit down and take your first bite; it's easier to get started.

~Deb Bollom, ADHD & Life Coach

Deb Bollom is a Professional Senior Certified ADHD and Life Coach working with ADHD adults and entrepreneurs who are stuck in details and overwhelm. www.d5coaching.com

Processing Styles

As no two of us have the same DNA, so no two of us have the same brain, and no two of us have the same ADHD. Part of that statement might be new information to you; however, I hope not. We are each unique individuals who do things in our own specific ways. One of the things we each do uniquely is process information. Some of the common processing styles are auditory, visual, verbal, cognitive, kinesthetic, tactile and intuitive.

When you discover how you uniquely process information, you open a new dimension of knowledge about yourself and discover a new set of tools. Students discover how to study so they better link information in their brains. Knowledge of processing styles also helps in relationships and in communication with partners, team members, customers, family and friends. If you're curious about your unique style, go to www.acktivv.com and find it out.

~Dee Shofner Doochin, MLAS, PCC, CMC, PACG, SCAC

Dee Shofner Doochin, MLAS; Professional Certified Coach; Certified Mentor Coach; Senior Certified ADHD Coach; wife, mother, grandmother, and great-grandmother with ADHD; adventurer; lover of life! www.deedoochin.com

Anxiety and ADHD: Problems x 2

Anxiety is an ADHD frequent flyer. It can mimic and compound the symptoms of ADHD. It can also be more debilitating that the ADHD itself.

Did you know that feeling chronically stressed or having chronic physical symptoms can actually be a sign of an anxiety disorder?

If you think you might have this issue, seek the help of a specialist. Specialists have greater expertise than non-specialists do. They reliably get better results for their anxiety-ridden patients. And the good news is that anxiety is highly treatable. Once your anxiety is under better control, you'll find it easier to be in action and take charge of both your ADHD and your life.

~Sarah D. Wright, M.S., A.C.T.

Nationally-known ADHD coach Sarah D. Wright specializes in helping professionals in small businesses get on track and get going. FocusForEffectiveness.com ~ Sarah@FocusForEffectiveness.com (858) 408-9338.

Rename the Game to WIN it!

Whenever you're stuck or spinning your wheels, ask, "How have I named the game that makes this difficult to do?" Remember, The Name of the Game™ determines how you play - and your subconscious never sleeps. When you name the game something like "clean up the house," how will you know when you're done? No matter what you tell yourself aloud, your subconscious equates "clean" with "spotless." Nobody's eager to play a game they can't win. With "spend 2 hours cleaning," the problem becomes picking and prioritizing. Renaming beats rumination. Start with *why* you are cleaning today, then add today's deadline. "Mom will be here in two hours, and I want to avoid another lecture," is an instant focuser. The importance of de-cluttering and cleaning things that Mom always notices becomes clear — even if it means you stash the kids' mess under their beds for now. Rename your games to trigger ACTION.

~Madelyn Griffith-Haynie, CTP, CMC, A.C.T., MCC, SCAC

Madelyn Griffith-Haynie, multi-certified ADD coaching field co-founder, has been helping clients and coaches rename their games for 25 years. www.ADDandSoMuchMore.com ~ mgh@addcoach.com

Just Say "Poor Baby"

Sometimes, we parents talk too much. We want to teach our kids, or have them listen to us, so we drone on and on, sounding like Charlie Brown's teacher. When kids are dealing with life, and we're focused on the teachable moment, we rob them of the opportunity to experience the emotion of the event itself. One of our teenagers, being the self-advocator that years of special needs schooling has taught her to be, recently started saying, "poor baby." That is short for, "Mom, don't lecture me now, please, I just need you to say poor baby and rub my back." She is not rude or sarcastic. She is asking for what she needs. As parents, it's hard to let go of learning opportunities! But the pay-off of emotional support is worth it. If you need help, call us. We understand, and will respond with an authentic "poor baby!"

~ Elaine Taylor-Klaus, CPCC, ACC, and
Diane Dempster, MHSA, CPC, ACC

ImpactADHD helps parents help kids. Elaine Taylor-Klaus & Diane Dempster provide reality-based training, with coaching to make it stick. We help your family thrive! http://www.ImpactADHD.com

Jump-Start Your Creative Process

People with ADHD are extremely creative; however, the tendency toward perfectionism often sabotages their creativity. Remember this: The main difference between a professional and an amateur is that the professional consistently moves forward. Here are some tips to help jump-start your creative process:

- Carve out a sacred time for yourself -- no distractions!

- Turn this time into a daily ritual.

- Set achievable goals. If 15 minutes feels right initially, go with that. (Congratulate yourself if you do more.)

- Let your creativity flow; edit later.

- If you feel blocked, don't beat yourself up. Try journaling. Writing about the thoughts in your head, in the moment, can actually help push through your creative block.

- Stay positive; don't second-guess your creative process.

- Life can get crazy; if you miss a day, give yourself a break without judgment.

~Michael Frolichstein, MFA

Michael Frolichstein, MFA, is a Filmmaker and Life Coach specializing in ADHD and creativity. You can find me at mwfcoaching.com or email me mwfcoaching@gmail.com.

The Writing is on the Mirror

When I want to remember something, I start with a well established habit. Two times each and every day, I stand before my bathroom mirror: my launch pad. I write lists, reminders and affirmations right on the mirror with a marker, which never leaves the bathroom counter. Urgent or important items are written in the middle, where I can't miss them. My "shower thoughts" are easily jotted there before they are forgotten. Everything is there, right in front of me.

In the same way I use the bathroom mirror, I use my car's dashboard. I have a notepad with lightweight card stock pages, where I write my "car thoughts," errands and reminders. I put those notes front and center, right in front of my tachometer (which I have no use for anyway). What part of your every day routine can you use as your foundation for success?

~Mindy Schwartz Katz, MS, ACC

Mindy Schwartz Katz, ADHD/Life Coach, helps ADDers get over, around and through obstacles that get in the way of living their unique life. www.yourlife-planb.com ~ mindy@yourlife-planb.com

Weaknesses Need Not Apply

Using your strengths can help improve your overall effectiveness more than trying to correct your weaknesses. Reflect on your strengths by answering the following questions.

1.   What went well yesterday?
2.   What did you do well to make yesterday's success happen?
3.   How can you make yesterday's success happen today?
4.   What do you love to do?
5.   How can you apply your passion to your goals?
6.   What comes easy to you?
7.   How would a co-worker, client or friend describe your strengths? (Not sure? Ask them!)

After you have answered the questions, make a list of all the strengths that come to mind. Aim to identify at least 10 strengths. Keep the list close to you, especially when developing action plans to achieve your goals.

~Laura Rolands, ADHD Coach

Laura Rolands is an ADHD Coach who helps clients manage time, focus on priorities, pay attention, increase productivity and achieve goals. Learn more at www.MyAttentionCoach.com.

Helpful Habits: "Little Lists"

Many adults with AD/HD rely on an effective strategy of daily to-do lists and reminder notes conveniently posted at home, in the car, at work. *"Little Lists"* are equally important. That is, lists for the little ones in your life, including the young ones who cannot read yet.

When my children were little, the school mornings were such a struggle, especially in the winter. I would call out a litany of repeat reminders until the necessary items, including the seasonal mittens, hats, boots, and scarves were finally on. It was an exhausting routine.

In a moment of insight, it dawned on me that my children could draw/color their own list -- their very own *"Little List,"* created by them, and for them, posted at their eye level where they could refer to it for themselves.

And it worked..."*Little Lists.*"

~*Monika Pompetzki, ADHD Coach*

Monika Pompetzki, BSc, MEd, AD/HD, academic, & life coach, focused on creating HELPFUL HABITS that can make life a little easier. www.add-adhdCoaching.com ~ (905) 336-8330 ~ monika@add-adhdCoaching.com

Attention is Energy

Young children do not measure the value of attention based on whether it is positive or negative. A child measures the value of attention they are receiving based on the energy associated with that attention. Little ones with ADHD cannot always discriminate between good and bad. But they can tell the difference between high and low energy levels.

We often use a much higher volume voice and energy output when reprimanding our children, and a lower level volume voice and energy output when praising our children. If our negative response holds more energy than our positive response, than the negative reaction will be what our child seeks. Change your dance and put more energy into your positive responses. You will begin to see more positive behaviors from your child.

~Judith Champion, MSW, ACG

Judith Champion, MSW, ACG, ADHD Family Coach and Educator, ADHD Associates. judith@judithchampion.com ~ www.ADHDAssociates.com ~ (609) 468-0819

Choose and Move

Most of us have so many things we want and need to be doing that the ideas can get to swirling in our heads to the point where we can't decide and just shut down. Think of each item you have to do as a small boulder that you want to move a mile down the road. You may have 100 small boulders that need moving. Now, you have a choice: Grab one boulder and move it a foot, grab the next one and move it a foot, and so on down the line. Working that way, you really can get all 100 boulders moved a foot toward your goal. How does that feel? Your other choice is to grab one boulder – any one will do – and carry it 1/2 mile or the whole way. Set it down and notice how you feel. Do you notice more energy and momentum? The key is to choose and get moving.

~Barbara Luther, Master Certified Coach

Barbara Luther, President, Professional Association of ADHD Coaches, www.PAACCoaches.org. Director of Training, ADD Coach Academy, www.addca.com. Master Certified ADHD Coach.
www.WindBeneathYourWings.com ~ www.SoaringCoachesCircle.com
St. Louis, MO ~ 573-340-3559

Who is Your Tribe?

One of my favorite things to do is take my dogs to the community dog park. When they are there, the dogs seem to be in a world with a language and behavior all their own. They know how to greet one another in friendly dog fashion, can judge how much sniffing is enough, recognize how much tussling or chasing is good, and understand that getting too excited or barking too much is not allowed. They are home among their "tribe." You may not know this, but people with ADHD are a tribe. There are others just like you whose brains are full of ideas, who understand that inner restlessness and often have no idea what time it is! Being with our tribe, with people that understand us, is incredibly important if you have ADHD. You can find members of your tribe online and at conferences by going to:

- CHADD.org
- ADD.org
- ADDresources.com

~Laurie Dupar, PMHNP, RN, PCC Certified ADHD Coach and Nurse Practitioner

Laurie Dupar is an internationally-recognized ADHD coach, specializing in people newly diagnosed with ADHD. (916) 791-1799 ~ www.coachingforadhd.com

Master Your Unique Operating System

I work with college students who design brains for space ships. In my coaching peer mentoring classes, they have been empowered to discover and engineer the perfect fuel and structure for optimum power of their unique neurobiological brain wiring.

They have discovered that eating dessert first works, as well as getting their turbo brain fired up with passion, interest and intent by doing what is most fulfilling first and then riding the wave of exhilaration through more tedious necessities necessary to fulfill their goals. They often utilize an accountability buddy or a body double, music, etc. The key is that they create the perfect engineering strategy for maximizing the potential of their ADHD brain and nervous system.

~Nancy Anne Brighton, LCSW, ADHD Coach

Nancy Anne Brighton, LCSW, ADHD Coach, empowers gifted adults with upside-down brilliance to create compelling futures from the future. Bright Brains Building. Brighter Future. www.BrightONBrains.com ~ ADHDcoach@BrightonBrains.com ~ (386) 290-6703

Drop Your Drawers!

Drop your kids' drawers, too. Open up time and space by hanging your laundry; AFTER it's clean, of course. The oldest of "children," including spouses, are often challenged with maintaining order in dressers and closets. Instead of being sentenced to a life of sorting, folding and straightening, simply arm yourself with an arsenal of quality hangers and conquer those piles. Doing this task right out of the dryer will save you from the wrinkles (and you will look sharp too).

Getting resistance? Try it. Many a mate has surrendered after quickly and successfully finding that special t-shirt or pair of pants. Undershirts? Hang them, too. Boxers and bras? Pass. Need more hanging space? If finances allow, redesign your closet with a second rod. Or, for less than $20, pick up an additional hang rod that is made to hang from your existing rod.

~Nancy Bean, Certified ADHD Coach,
Professional Organizer, Interior Designer

Nancy Bean builds relationships between people, places and spaces, helping clients create change in their lives. SIMPLIFY by DESIGN: Certified ADHD Coach, Designer/Organizer. simplify@nancybean.com

The 7-Step PowerPlan to Success™
Step #1: Cultivate Self-Awareness

Take a realistic inventory of your strengths and challenges: Who you are... and aren't, what you are likely to do... or not. Avoid sugar-coating things, but also acknowledge all you *have* accomplished, even if not quite up to your sometimes overly-critical standards of what you 'should' be able to do.

Think about the things you do well, your talents and areas of competency. Be mindful of what 'gets you going' AND what 'shuts you down,' and how this impacts your self-identity and relationships with others. There are many coaching exercises that help with this process.

Without self-awareness, you risk designing a life that may look good conceptually, but doesn't work for *you*. **When you know *who* you are and *how* you function (or not), you can develop effective strategies** that work with your strengths and compensate for your challenges **to create a life that fits!**

~Susan Lasky, MA, BCC, SCAC

Susan Lasky, Master ADD/ADHD Strategist, Productivity Coach & Professional Organizer, creator of the 7-Step PowerPlan to Success™ and the 28-Day Accountability Challenge™. www.SusanLasky.com ~ www.PowerPlanToSuccess.com ~ Susan@SusanLasky.com

Clean Out the Refrigerator First

Just prior to Thanksgiving, many of us head to the store to purchase a big turkey. We navigate through the crowds and find the perfect one. Delighted, we rush home ready to jump on other holiday tasks. Then we discover that we forgot a minor detail: the refrigerator is packed with other foods and there's no room for the turkey. The refrigerator has to be cleaned out first. We didn't allow time for that, and now we're going to fall behind on everything else.

This little drama, repeated in home after home each year, holds a great lesson for those of us with ADHD trying to shoehorn one more thing into our busy lives: it's difficult to find time to address new opportunities when we don't have any room in our lives to fit them in. Better to clear out the refrigerator first, so we have some room to operate.

~Paul O'Connor, MCC

Paul O'Connor coaches business executives with ADHD. He is a Master Certified Coach, secretary of the Professional Association of ADHD Coaches, based in Atlanta. (404) 377-4712 paul@EnergyForLifeCoach.com ~ www.EnergyForLifeCoach.com

Use a "30's Workout" to Get In and Out of the Gym Fast

Here's a workout that capitalizes on the very best of the ADHD brain by emphasizing structure and a sense of urgency.

For the 30's Workout, you'll need a sports watch with an interval timer. Even better, get a free interval training app for your smartphone. Set your timer to beep every 30 seconds. Make your way to a chest machine or dumbbells, or drop to the floor for push-ups. When the timer sounds, start your exercise, picking a weight and intensity you can maintain for 30 seconds. When the round is over, you have 30 seconds to make your way to the next station and get ready (beep!) for a shoulder exercise. Continue alternating 30-second bursts of moderate intensity resistance training with 30-second rest periods, moving on quickly to a back exercise. Then abs, quads, hamstrings, biceps, and triceps.

Move through these 8 stations a second time. You're done!

~Dr. Nowell, Ph.D.

Dr. Nowell is a Neuropsychologist offering workshops and clinical services. Contact him at www.DrNowell.com to set up a one-hour ADHD Q & A consultation.

You are a "Do-er" verses a "Be-er"

People with ADHD have many innate qualities; one of these is that "doing" comes naturally. If you are an entrepreneur, taking action, making those small steps to get your business off the ground is a natural gift. You welcome productivity, creating your next product or planning your next marketing approach. Harnessing this affinity for action or "doing" is a key secret to your enjoying business success.

Being the owner of your own business requires a tremendous amount of mental, emotional and physical energy. By tapping into this personal ADHD action source, you are able to put in the extra hours, pull those all-nighters or meet those last-minute deadlines.

Being an emerging entrepreneur may include having limited funds, but it also includes unlimited energy!

~Laurie Dupar, PMHNP, RN, PCC Certified ADHD Coach and Nurse Practitioner

Laurie Dupar is a senior certified ADHD Coach and trained nurse practitioner. You can reach her at www.coachingforadhd.com or (916) 791-1799.

Understanding How

Life is a challenge for everyone. Believing in yourself makes things possible, not easy. But by educating yourself and getting treatment for your ADHD, you can take your own steps to success. Start by taking baby steps: read, talk to others, or build a support group. When you learn to take charge, triumph is just another small baby step away.

~Dulce Torres, LPC-S, BCC, ADHD Coach

Dulce Torres, Licensed Professional Counselor/Supervisor, Board Certified Coach, specializes in ADHD coaching that helps teenagers, adults, and parents to find their hidden strengths. www.dstcoaching.com ~ dtorres@dstcoaching.com

The 7-Step PowerPlan to Success™
Step #2: Accept Yourself
"I 'yam what I 'yam"

Accept who you are, how you think, and the way you do (or don't) do things. Let go of how you think you 'should' be. You are who you are (personality, history, ADD, LD, IQ, EQ, types of intelligence, co-existing mental or physical issues, birth order, astrological sign, Chinese birth year animal... you get the idea). *As Popeye the Sailorman said, "I 'yam what I 'yam."*

When we truly accept ourselves, warts and all, we open our minds to new ways of being. Instead of reacting, we are better able to act. This is critical, as when we're in reaction mode, our brain is in 'fight or flight' mode, viewing any intervention or change – even positive ones, as a threat to our way of being. Be kind to yourself and gain the ability and energy to create a life you love!

~Susan Lasky, MA, BCC, SCAC

Susan Lasky, Master ADD/ADHD Strategist, Productivity Coach & Professional Organizer, creator of the 7-Step PowerPlan to Success™ and the 28-Day Accountability Challenge™. www.SusanLasky.com ~ www.PowerPlanToSuccess.com ~ Susan@SusanLasky.com

Giant Monthly Calendars for Visual and Kinesthetic People!

I had a hard time planning and organizing myself. I used to be late to my appointments, forget them entirely or sometimes I had two meetings at the same time. This is even harder when you have your own business and no secretary! I'm a visual person, and I need to see the whole month in order to process cognitively, prioritize things and make my plan. I have designed a simple calendar, 120 x 100 cm, which I stick on my wall in my office. It just shows one month. I can write and draw on it. Then I copy it to my iPad! Because I am visual and kinesthetic, I can remember the meetings and other stuff. It also stops me from overloading myself. I can see my potential in order to create breaks and rewards. I really benefit from this monthly wall calendar as a visual and kinesthetic person!

~Eda Aydogan, MA, ACC, PACG

Eda Aydogan, MA, ACC, PACG, ADHD Coach, specializes in helping you understand your own ADHD and find coping strategies. For more information, find me at www.dehbka.com. eaydogan@dehbka.com

"That some achieve great success, is proof to all that others can achieve it as well."

~ Abraham Lincoln

The 7-Step PowerPlan to Success™
Step #3: Decide You Can!

Until we believe that what we want is truly possible, we can't effect real change or create new ways of being. We always have the power of choice, which means taking personal responsibility and getting out of the blame game; our problems may be compounded by biology, history, environment, experiences or even the other people in our lives, but we can still choose how we respond to any situation. Let go of the guilt trap of being overly self-critical, which keeps us caught in a web of failure and regret (or even perfectionism), instead of allowing us to move forward in action. We aren't perfect, but we can choose to make changes that transform the way we think, work and live! As Henry Ford said, "Whether you think you can, or think you can't – you're right."

~Susan Lasky, MA, BCC, SCAC

Susan Lasky, Master ADD/ADHD Strategist, Productivity Coach & Professional Organizer, creator of the 7-Step PowerPlan to Success™ and the 28-Day Accountability Challenge™. www.SusanLasky.com ~ www.PowerPlanToSuccess.com ~ Susan@SusanLasky.com

Before You Speak, THINK...

As a person with ADHD, one of my biggest issues was speaking without thinking and not hearing what I was saying when I was angry or upset. This behavior had affected my relationship with my family and with my friends. I suffered a lot until I learned to think before I speak. Now, when I am upset or mad at something, I remind myself of the Indian Guru Sai Baba's famous quote:

"Before you speak, think: Is it necessary? Is it true? Is it kind? Will it hurt anyone? Will it improve on the silent?"

~Pınar Kobaş, ADHD Expert

Pınar Kobaş, Mental Health Counselor and ADHD Expert with ADHD. She lives in Turkey. www.dehbka.com ~ pkobas@dehbka.com

What Most People Don't Get About the Obvious

A few thoughts to get the wheels turning:

1. What is obvious is a function of what you attend to! Example: How many seconds are there in a year? Twelve, right? January 2nd, February 2nd, March 2nd, etc.

2. If the obvious solution isn't working, there's a good chance you are attending to the wrong thing. Example: The organizational solution isn't working. Why isn't it working? Because while you may be similar to the person for whom it worked before, you are not the same. You are different, so find a different solution that works!

~Jeff Copper, MBA, PCC, ACG, CPCC

Jeff Copper, MBA, PCC, ACG, CPCC, is an attention coach, founder of DIG Coaching Practice, and host of Attention Talk Radio...Your ADHD Information Station! www.digcoaching.com

Creatively Organized: Another Way to Do Things

Following are a few of my best organization tips:

• Learn the art of letting go: if you don't need, use, or desire a particular item, let it go. If you think you may need it again one day decide what you can use as a substitute.

• If you have too much stuff ask: "What is enough?"

• Greeting card clutter: recycle the cards signed by people you don't know. Do the same with cards signed with just a name. Save one or two cards from those you love or who love you like crazy.

• One notebook for all notes, one calendar for all appointments. Find one of each that works for you. If what you choose doesn't work, try something else!

~Dr. Regina Lark, Ph.D., CPO

Dr. Regina Lark, Certified Professional Organizer, specializes in de-cluttering and organizing for the ADD/ADHD brain. www.AClearPath.net ~ regina@AClearPath.net

Awesome Qualities of ADHD

Life with ADHD is a 24-hour, 7-day-a-week adventure! Unfortunately, the majority of focus on ADHD is on the "negative" aspects that people with ADHD experience. Rarely are the positive attributes of ADHD celebrated. Here are some that I hope you appreciate about yourself!

- Brain surfer
- Out of the box thinker
- Creative
- Fun to be with
- Sees details others miss
- Innovative
- Humorous
- Inspiring
- Resourceful
- Highly sensitive
- Musically intuitive
- Adventurous
- Intelligent
- Can talk...a bit
- Multi-tasker
- Able to live in the moment
- Willing to take risks
- High energy

~Laurie Dupar, ADHD Coach & Expert

Laurie Dupar is an internationally-recognized ADHD expert. Find out more about your *Brain Surfing & 31 other Awesome Qualities of ADHD* at www.coachingforadhd.com.

If All Else Fails, Go for a Walk

Sometimes I find that I don't know what to do next. There are papers to deal with in the office, plenty of to-do lists, and dust sparkling on the bookshelves, but none of it grabs my attention nearly strongly enough to engage me in activity. As soon as I realize I've been rotating on the spot for several minutes, I put on my trainers and go for a walk. It's my what-to-do-if-all-else-fails rule.

Why? Outside is just so **loud** compared to inside; it lifts your activation level instantly. There's traffic, other people, and things happening not under your immediate control. Walking gets your blood flowing and your brain miraculously able to think again. Before you realize it, you're planning what to do next.

And walking brings unexpected bonuses: the smell of honeysuckle in a neighbor's garden, a perfect full moon. And spectacular calf muscles.

~Dr. Gillian Hayes, Ph.D.

Gillian Hayes, PhD, is an ADHD coach who specializes in helping students, academics and other high achievers dig out their best. gillian@brightshinycoaching.com

The 7-Step PowerPlan to Success™ Step #4: Clarify Your Goals & Prioritize

Now that you are aware of who you are, have accepted yourself and believe you have the power to make changes in your life, decide *what* you want to change. Choose specific goals to work toward. Trying to do too much (our natural tendency) is setting yourself up for failure.

Clarify specific objectives and avoid goals that are too broad. Instead of thinking, "I am going to master time," start with "I am going to get out of the house by 7:30 a.m.," or "I will exercise 3 times per week." Those goals are specific and measureable. You can accomplish them (or at least get better at them) and move on to another goal. Prioritize your goals by what is important (watching out for distractions), and make sure to include goals that bring you joy.

~Susan Lasky, MA, BCC, SCAC

Susan Lasky, Master ADD/ADHD Strategist, Productivity Coach & Professional Organizer, creator of the 7-Step PowerPlan to Success™ and the 28-Day Accountability Challenge™. www.SusanLasky.com ~ www.PowerPlanToSuccess.com ~ Susan@SusanLasky.com

20 Seconds of Bravery is all it Takes

What you avoid tends to run your life, but you only need 20 seconds of true bravery to overcome obstacles. To risk embarrassment, or potential danger, 20 seconds can change everything. When we avoid something, we give it power and control over us. But usually, our fear is worse than the reality. To avoid discomfort and disappointment, we don't set limits, make requests, or talk to our kids about drugs & alcohol. But when we do, when we bravely stand up to ourselves (and our fears), the short-term discomfort loses to the long-term gains. Try practicing mini-episodes of bravery. Start difficult conversations, make unpopular requests, set clear limits and stand firm in your resolve. Think about one thing you've been avoiding, take a deep breath, and tackle it square on. You can do it. The bravery part only takes about 20 seconds!

~ Elaine Taylor-Klaus, CPCC, ACC, and
Diane Dempster, MHSA, CPC, ACC

ImpactADHD helps parents help kids. Elaine Taylor-Klaus & Diane Dempster provide reality-based training, with coaching to make it stick. We help your family thrive! http://www.ImpactADHD.com

Creatively Organized: Bedroom and Clothing

How to keep your bedroom organized:

• De-clutter your clothes by letting a friend help you decide what looks great and not-so-great. Donate the stuff you don't need, want, desire. Be passionate about your choices of what to keep.

• Consider bedroom walls as perfect real estate to hang your clothing. Purchase fun hooks - bold and colorful in a variety of shapes and sizes. Dot the walls with hooks and let your clothes hang there rather than inside a closet.

• Instead of folding or piling onto any flat surface, use colorful baskets for bras, underwear, and socks.

• Shoe bags with clear pockets are perfect for your jewelry, hair or nail accessories.

• Store bed linens by placing folded top and bottom sheets and one pillowcase into the second pillow case of a sheet set.

• Remember, for every hour you spend de-cluttering, you need an hour to put away what you keep.

~Dr. Regina Lark, Ph.D., CPO

Dr. Regina Lark, Certified Professional Organizer, specializes in de-cluttering and organizing for the ADD/ADHD brain. www.AClearPath.net ~ regina@AClearPath.net

Invite John Amos Comenius into Your Home

My old Education professor claimed the motto: "A place for everything and everything in its place," was first written by John Amos Comenius, known as the Father of Education in the 17th Century. When doing his rounds, my professor often called on him when he saw an untidy desk or classroom.

Fast forward 40 years!

When I moved into a smaller house, I was determined to keep it tidy and called upon John Amos for help. I framed a lovely portrait of him and hung it in my vestibule, so his is the first face I see when I enter. His stern eyes follow me, making sure I hang my keys on the doorknob, place my wallet in the basket, hang my coat in the cupboard, and leave my boots by the door. Now I need to invite him into other parts of the house.

~Jane Patrick, BA, MEd.

Jane Patrick, retired teacher, diagnosed with ADD at age 75. Now enjoying the trip! Advocate for neglected group of 60+ ADDers. janeham@abacom.com

Study Better with White Noise

How many parents have hollered, "Turn off that music and do your homework!"? Background noise is typically thought of as hindering the ability to pay attention, but for students with "inattentive" ADHD, a moderate level of white noise can actually help.* If drifting is your problem, play your favorite instrumental music in the background (lyrics can be distracting) or try white noise. A fan can do the trick. You can also go digital with Ambiance (www.ambianceapp.com) or WhiteNoise (www.tmsoft.com), available for both computer and smart phone. Remember: be thoughtful of others. Keep the volume low, or use headphones when you're plugged in. Here's an added bonus: if you're a light sleeper, white noise can also help you fall and stay asleep.

* Soderlund, G, Sikstrom, S, Loftesnes, J, Sonuga-Barke, E. (2010). The effects of background white noise on memory performance in inattentive school children. *Behavioral and Brain Functions*, 6:55.

~Roland Rotz, Ph.D. & Sarah D. Wright, M.S.

Roland Rotz, Ph.D., and Sarah D. Wright, M.S., are authors of *Fidget to Focus*, a handbook of strategies for living more easily with ADHD. www.FidgetToFocus.com

"I Know Her, Her Name is . . . Oh, Crap!"

Situation: I have a terrible time remembering names, even when I've known someone for five years. Then I have to either avoid the person or just pray the name will come before I embarrass myself.

Strategy: Making good use of your cell phone can help. I was recently at a business event and saw a very important person walk into the room. As she was saying her hello's and making her way toward me, I started to panic. Then I remembered the company she worked for and discreetly looked it up in my cell phone. There it was: her name, her husband's name, and other business and personal information. Whether personal or business, enter new names into your cell phone, noting their birthday, spouse's name, children, recent events in their life and more. You could also do this on a 3x5 card and before contacting someone, review your note card.

~Joyce Kubik, ADHD Coach, CC (IAC)

Joyce Kubik, Certified Life and ADHD Coach for students and adults, author of planning journals developed specifically for ADHD. Find it and more at www.bridgetosuccess.net.

It's Habit Forming!

It's hard enough to do all the things that we have to do without adding yet one more thing to our established routines. When you want to remember something new or out of the ordinary, it is often helpful to pair the thing that you want to remember with something that is more automatic. You might place the new medication next to the coffee pot so you'll see it in the morning. Put the library books by your purse or briefcase so you'll avoid yet more overdue fines. Plug in the phone charger near where you keep your glasses so you will remember to take the phone when you leave the house. (Extra points if you remember your glasses, too!) It's better than a string tied around your finger!

For more information, go to www.FocusForEffectiveness.com/blog.

~Roxanne Fouche, ADHD Coach

Roxanne Fouche, ADHD Coach, helps both students and women live successfully with ADHD and related challenges. In person, phone, or Skype. Contact (858) 484-4749 or Roxanne@FocusForEffectiveness.com.

6 Steps to Taming Your ADHD Gremlin

I have found that ADHD gremlins (our negative self-talk) have positive intentions and serve a purpose in our personal transformation. Their true messages can be difficult to understand when they show up in our daily lives, holding us back and getting in the way of our success.

Play along and explore how your gremlin is showing up:

1. What is the gremlin telling you? Write it on a piece of paper.
2. What does the gremlin look like? Perhaps you want to draw a picture of it.
3. You can also give it a name.
4. The gremlin has a positive intention – what does it really want for you?
5. How can you achieve that?
6. What did you learn from this?

By becoming aware of our gremlins, we can take back the power and learn new ways to be who we truly are.

~Charlotte Hjorth, ADHD Coach, PCC

Charlotte Hjorth, Certified ADHD Coach, PCC - Supervisor, Trainer, Speaker, Writer and Blogger - Initiator and Campaign Leader of ADHD Awareness Week Denmark since 2008. www.ADHDkompagniet.com

Sound Like an Expert Every Time You Open Your Mouth!

We blurt out thoughts without preparing. Impulsive, we have to be sure we express our valuable contributions clearly. Or we just want to get our "two cents" in before the subject changes!

• Before adding something to a conversation, STOP, imagine how your audience thinks and how to help them understand your idea (use their jargon, etc.).
• Keep a small notebook or sheet of paper to record your thoughts, or dictate your notes into your telephone.
• Write down your thoughts, and reconsider them before speaking.
• Make brief notes on how you might present your ideas.
• Wait for a lull in the conversation.
• If the time has passed and the subject is no longer in discussion, keep your notes and use them later if needed.

People will await your every intelligent word!

~ Hervé J. LeBoeuf, III, Ph.D.

Dr. LeBoeuf, Life and ADHD Coach, believes people with ADHD of all ages can be successful by learning to work with their unique brains. HLeBoeuf@Gmail.com

"I've failed over and over again in my life and that is why I succeed."

~ Michael Jordan

The 7-Step PowerPlan to Success™
Step #5: Strategize for Success

Develop the strategies that will enable you to compensate, conquer and excel. Be a detective. Explore what has worked and what hasn't. Build on your strengths. Read, or listen to the audio versions of, some of the wonderful books and articles on ADD/ADHD, organization, time management, productivity, self-care, self-empowerment, etc. Visualize the benefits to help create the best path to achieving your goals.

Realize that you will need two types of strategies. It isn't enough to have strategies, tools and techniques to accomplish a task (the "doing"). You will also need them to get motivated to begin, to remain focused on the task and to stay with it until completion (the "getting it done"). For individualized help, support and accountability, one of the best investments you can make is to spend some time working with an experienced ADHD coach.

~Susan Lasky, MA, BCC, SCAC

Susan Lasky, Master ADD/ADHD Strategist, Productivity Coach & Professional Organizer, creator of the 7-Step PowerPlan to Success™ and the 28-Day Accountability Challenge™. www.SusanLasky.com ~ www.PowerPlanToSuccess.com ~ Susan@SusanLasky.com

When You Say NO, What are You Saying YES to?

People with ADHD can find themselves saying, "yes" before they have taken the time to consider the consequences. Because time is a finite resource, for every "yes" that we offer, we are naturally saying "no" to something else. "Yes, I'll be on the committee" means "no" to a few hours of family time; "yes" to one project means "no" to a different activity that has more potential or is more interesting. To break the habit of automatically saying "yes," pause between someone's request and your response so that you have time to think it through. You might say, "Hmm, interesting idea. I'll get back to you on that." Although it's nice to be agreeable and to be considered a team player, sometimes "no" is the best response. When you say "no," you are giving yourself the opportunity – and the permission - to say "yes" to something that is more important to you.

~Roxanne Fouche, ADHD Coach

Roxanne Fouche, ADHD Coach, helps both students and women live successfully with ADHD and related challenges. In person, phone, or Skype. Contact (858) 484-4749 or Roxanne@FocusForEffectiveness.com.

Coffee Pot Alarm Clocks

Like many people in college, waking up and getting out of bed for morning classes can be a near impossibility. Setting traditional alarms often fail. One innovative ADHD college student came up with his own way of making sure he didn't miss any of his morning classes. Each night, he would prepare the coffee and set the automatic timer to go off in the morning. Then he would set his alarm by his bed to go off five minutes before the coffee pot. His fail-proof system? When he made the coffee, he made sure that the coffee carafe was not under the coffee maker. If he didn't get up shortly after his bedside alarm went off, the coffee would end up all over the floor! According to him, it never failed. What are some of your favorite innovative solutions?

~Laurie Dupar, ADHD Coach & Expert

Laurie is a Senior Certified ADHD Coach with a special interest in working with college students. Reach her at www.coachingforadhd.com or (916) 791-1799.

Motivator Money

Tired of the feeling of not being able to get started and want a positive way to get things done? Why not find something you really would like to have and make that your motivation? Maybe it is a new smart phone that you have to earn by rewarding yourself when large tasks or goals are achieved. The way that works is that for each task or project you complete on time, you "earn" a set amount, say $20, to put into your bank towards your target reward. Once your bank account has enough for your purchase, you get to make it yours. Don't forget to celebrate and then set a new target reward.

~Deb Bollom, ADHD & Life Coach

Deb Bollom is a Professional Senior Certified ADHD and Life Coach working with ADHD adults and entrepreneurs who are stuck in details and overwhelm. www.d5coaching.com

ADHD Relationship Coaching: When One Partner has ADHD

Imagine this scenario: The spouse that does not have ADHD writes a list of specific brands of foods and cleaning products and sends the ADHD spouse to the supermarket. The ADHD spouse comes back with 10 bags but few things that he/she was supposed to buy and mostly the wrong brands!

Another scenario: The ADHD spouse is supposed to clean the garage over a specific period of time. He/she spends hours in the garage but instead of cleaning and throwing away what is regarded as "trash" by the non-ADHD spouse, he/she goes through everything and, being unable to throw anything away, makes even a bigger mess than before!

Relationship coaching helps the couples to successfully navigate these daily conflicts that, if left untreated, could dismantle a marriage or a relationship.

~Roya Kravetz, ACC, BCC, CMC

Roya Kravetz, Credentialed and Board-Certified Life Coach, Certified Executive Coach, Instructor and Speaker specializing in ADHD Family & Relationship Coaching.
www.adhdsuccesscoaching.com ~ (858) 334-8584

Tame the Email Monster

Does email often take over your day? Use these simple strategies to reduce the time you spend managing email.

1. Schedule time to review email only a few times each day. When you check your email all day long, you lose time transitioning between your current task and your emails. I found a 50% reduction in the time spent on email when I implemented this strategy.

2. You can also close your email program when you finish reviewing email at your designated time so you are not tempted to check on something, "just for a second." This will help you build your new habit of only checking email a few times each day.

3. My final recommendation is to delete an email as soon as possible after reviewing it so it does not clutter your inbox.

With these simple strategies, you increase your odds against the "email monster!"

~Laura Rolands, ADHD Coach

Laura Rolands is an ADHD Coach who helps clients manage time, focus on priorities, pay attention, increase productivity and achieve goals. Learn more at www.MyAttentionCoach.com

Give Your Brain the Day Off!

Give yourself ONE day to relax. You can have the whole rest of the week to worry about and solve whatever needs to be attended to, but take this one day to not think about any of that. Every now and then, children, as well as adults, need time to recharge, to reconnect, to live. In my house, we call it a mental health day. Rent a movie, plan a picnic, go to the mountains or lake and give your brain a vacation. ADHD brains work constantly. Many of us are not good sleepers and if we have nothing good to think about, we worry. Why? Because our brains just keep going! While your brain is on vacation, you are to be strict in requesting that none of your work, school, money, or other problems be allowed inside! All you are asking for is one day. See how invigorated you feel after.

~Sandy Alletto Corbin, MA, ACG, SCAC

Sandy Alletto Corbin, a Senior Credentialed ADHD Coach and teacher, woman with ADHD and a single mother of an ADHD daughter, specializes in coaching women, teens and college students and advocating for change. www.lifecoachsandyalletto.com

Memory Tips

Keep some colored dry erase markers by the bathroom mirror. Jot down grocery or to-do items when they pop into your head.

~Linda

Do You Know Your "Study Style"?

Many people know their "learning style:" they are either a visual, auditory, kinesthetic or tactile learner, or combination of these. However, knowing your "study style" or where, how and when you do your best homework, studying or learning is equally valuable. To figure out your "study style," ask yourself:

- Do I focus best in a quiet environment or where there is some background noise/activity?
- What music, pencil, pen, and lighting works best for me?
- Do I like to be able to move and stretch out or is sitting still less distracting?
- Do I like everything spread around me or do I pay attention better in a tidy environment?
- Do I learn best alone or with others?
- When do I do my "best"? In the morning/afternoon/early evening/night?

The answers to these questions can help you understand your best learning methods and your "study style."

~Laurie Dupar, ADHD Coach & Expert

Laurie Dupar, Senior Certified ADHD Coach and editor of *365+1 ways to succeed with ADHD*. www.CoachingforADHD.com
~ (916) 791-1799

Couples & ADHD: Everyone Needs to be Appreciated!

In many ADHD relationships, the non-ADHD partner can easily end up doing everything their ADHD partner forgets or neglects to do, including things like helping with kids, picking up dry cleaning, taking out the garbage, etc. After a while, the non-ADHD partner feels more like an overworked parent than a loving partner. Resentment and frustrations quickly build, tempers flare, intimacy fades and both partners end up feeling isolated and unappreciated. Begin showing appreciation by making a quick list of all the things your partner does for you. Consider what your life would be like if you had to do it all yourself! Let your partner know how grateful you are for all he/she does. Next, commit to doing something nice for your partner each week, to reinforce your appreciation. Let your actions say: "I love you and appreciate all that you do for me!"

~ Sarah A. Ferman, L.M.F.T., P.C.C.
& Robert L. Wilford, Ph.D.

Sarah Ferman, L.M.F.T., P.C.C., & Robert Wilford, Ph.D., are leading ADHD Couples Consultants, helping ADHD couples reconnect and create loving and enduring relationships. www.ADHDCouplesConsultants.com

"Passion First, Then Productivity"

You have probably heard that being interested in a task, idea, or conversation helps our ADHD brains to pay attention. When we aren't interested, then it's difficult to pay attention. In a way, it comes down to a numbers game. If we can be interested and engaged more than we're not, we'll have a higher likelihood of success. One way to stack the odds in our favor is to strategically identify things that we are passionate about and then work to increase the amount of time we spend in those areas. Look for areas in your work that line up with your passions and as you focus on those areas, you'll see a magical increase in your productivity as well as your enjoyment of the job. Remember: passion first, then productivity.

~Jay Carter, MBA, ACG

Jay Carter is an adult ADHD coach specializing in personal productivity and workplace issues. Learn more about Jay's practice at www.hyperfocusedcoaching.com or jaycarter@hyperfocusedcoaching.com.

It's Not Complicated

After much trial and error, there are a few practical tips that have really worked with my own son and others that I am honored to know. The omega vitamin capsules and drops for kids really do assist with concentration span, mood control and general well-being. Fruit smoothies are a great way to disguise anything they may not be willing to take. Organic food usually works best long-term, as they are very sensitive to stimuli in any form. I have learned that I should ask, not tell or command. I need to speak to and not at them. They normally have the answers to every question they ask and are just confirming that I have the right answer and that I understand it. Anything I do or say without purpose or meaning will be challenged. No two days are the same; expect to be surprised.

~Juliet Victor, Performance Coach

Juliet Victor, Certified Performance Coach specializing in transformation and behavioral coaching, and aspiring Consciousness Coach. Juliet.victor@vodamail.co.za

The 7-Step PowerPlan to Success™ Step #6: Take Action

Once you have strategies to accomplish specific objectives, you are ready to move into action. Unfortunately, knowing is not doing, and the ability to do what you have planned is at the heart of the ADHD challenge. That is why you have created strategies for both the doing and the getting it done. Stay mindful of prioritized goals and avoid low-priority tasks (which we often do first to avoid more challenging or boring tasks).

Remember steps 1 through 3 in the 7-Step PowerPlan to Success™ – Awareness that you are having a hard time, Acceptance that you are feeling this way, and Belief that it could be different. Then just do something to begin the process. Transition from thinking to doing in baby steps. Pick up the pen. Open the computer file. Pull out the folder. That small action transitions you to the activity. Then write one word, read one sentence, open the folder – you've made progress!

~Susan Lasky, MA, BCC, SCAC

Susan Lasky, Master ADD/ADHD Strategist, Productivity Coach & Professional Organizer, creator of the 7-Step PowerPlan to Success™ and the 28-Day Accountability Challenge™. www.SusanLasky.com ~ www.PowerPlanToSuccess.com ~ Susan@SusanLasky.com

Couples & ADHD: Give Yourself an Hour

Let's be honest; partners with ADHD seem to have a "magic" sense of time when it comes to getting to a destination. They magically believe that it will only take 10 minutes to get anywhere - 20 minutes tops! That belief might be true if they were are a Superhero or driving the Batmobile. A more down-to-earth approach is to accept your unrealistic ability to estimate travel time as part of your ADHD symptoms and apply the following principle. Allow yourself one hour to get to your destination. Mark your calendar, with a set time to leave an hour prior to your appointments. It may sound extreme at first, but you will be surprised to learn just how little "extra time" you have left when you factor in traffic, parking, distractions and other unforeseen circumstances. Arriving on time with no apology needed reduces your stress load!

~ Sarah A. Ferman, L.M.F.T., P.C.C.
& Robert L. Wilford, Ph.D.

Sarah Ferman, L.M.F.T., P.C.C., & Robert Wilford, Ph.D., are leading ADHD Couples Consultants, helping ADHD Couples reconnect and create loving and enduring relationships. www.ADHDCouplesConsultants.com

The Secret Behind Transforming a "Boring" Job to a Less Boring One

It is well known that individuals who are diagnosed with ADHD have a very hard time performing "boring" tasks. Therefore, I suggest that they try to combine the less interesting activities with interesting ones. Here are some suggestions:

- Listen to music while doing chores and/or homework.
- Find a buddy to go to the gym or take a walk with.
- Floss your teeth while watching a favorite show on T.V.
- Listen to a favorite book while on the treadmill or walking.
- Brush your teeth while taking a shower.
- Invite a few fun friends over to clean up the garage and/or the house.
- When doing filing and/or paperwork (boring tasks for individuals with ADHD), have a friend or colleague sit in the room with you performing their own tasks.

~Roya Kravetz, ACC, BCC, CMC

Roya Kravetz specializes in coaching youth and adults with ADHD, as well as educating and coaching parents regarding ADHD and/or related challenges.
www.adhdsuccesscoaching.com ~ (858) 334-8584

Re-Frame a Picture? NO, Re-Frame A Belief!

Re-framing is a great tool that I use with many clients. It involves changing the way you typically view a task, situation, whatever, to see it through a different set of glasses! It's a choice you choose to make. Example: Many graduate students I work with worry that they don't do homework like "normal" students because they like working late at night and early into the mornings. I ask if they are getting bad grade, missing classes? Typical answer: "No." This response is usually followed by, "Late night is when I get some of my best work done because it's quiet, nothing else is going on that distracts me, and I am ready to sit." To re-frame, I point out that this is "normal!" Why? Because it works! I ask, "Why not just change how you think about studying rather than change your whole study system?" Try this on today. Re-frame a belief!

~Sandy Alletto Corbin, MA, ACG, SCAC

Sandy Alletto Corbin, a Senior Credentialed ADHD Coach and teacher, woman with ADHD and a single mother of an ADHD daughter, specializes in coaching women, teens and college students and advocating for change. www.lifecoachsandyalletto.com

Improve Your Focus and Attention with a Simple Brain Exercise

Are you more scattered and distracted than you would like? Here's a simple at-home brain exercise to help you stay focused. Hold your thumb in front of your face and keep your eyes focused directly on your thumb while you walk around the room. Sit in a chair and then get up again, open a door, or pick something up from your desk and put it back down, *all while you keep your eyes locked on your thumb*!

This Thumb-Walk Exercise builds areas of your brain that keep you focused. Do this exercise for one or two minutes twice a day to improve your concentration with all kinds of activities including homework and remembering why you came into the room and what you were just talking about. You can watch a video demonstration of this and other brain-building exercises to help ADHD and Learning Disabilities at www.BrainTimeVideos.com.

~ Dr. Jim Otis, Fellow, American College of Functional Neurology

Dr. Otis specializes in drug-free treatment for ADHD and Learning Disabilities and is the inventor of BrainTime™, a patent-pending technology for optimal brain health. www.BrainTimeVideos.com

Minimizing Morning Madness

"Hurry up...let's get going...I can't believe we're late again!" Sound too familiar? Being frustrated, angry, upset or battling the way to the front door is not the way most families want to begin their day. Minimizing this morning madness takes some planning, ingenuity and patience. Here are some strategies to try:

- Have your student pick out two outfits the night before. They can choose one of them to wear in the morning.
- Give your child their medication a half hour to an hour before they need to get up. It will get their brain engaged earlier.
- Let them be responsible for getting out of bed.
- Create a "launch pad" for each person.
- Agree on a special treat, such as stopping for bagels, if everyone gets up and out on time.

Minimize morning madness and everyone's day will start off better!

~Laurie Dupar, ADHD Coach & Expert

Laurie Dupar is a trained Psychiatric Mental Health Nurse Practitioner and Senior Certified ADHD Coach. Reach her at www.coachingforadhd.com or (916) 791-1799.

Managing Relationships

Relationships can be hard when you have ADHD. Your lack of follow-through not only affects you but now also your partner. Letting down your partner feels terrible inside when you have not carried out a promise to do or complete something. Also, your working memory problems sometimes cause you to not remember important conversations or agreements. You don't *choose* to let your partner down or not to meet them halfway. It is your neurochemistry at work. What to do?

1) *Don't* blame it on the ADHD and leave it at that

2) *Don't* get defensive; you can work this out

3) *Do* make sure you and your partner have a good understanding of ADHD

4) *Do* come up with a plan that focuses on your strengths, not your weaknesses

5) *Do* have a back-up plan

6) *Do* make sure both of you keep your sense of humor intact during this process

~Abigail Wurf, M.Ed., CLC

Abigail Wurf, M.Ed., CLC, is trained to coach couples and individuals alike who are affected by ADHD. Serving Washington DC and nationally. awurf@verizon.net ~ abigailwurf.com ~ (202) 244-2234

Couples & ADHD: Five Things First!

For partners with ADHD, there is a tremendous satisfaction that comes with actually getting things done in the relationship. The challenge is that the days can quickly become a whirlwind of tasks that never seem to get completed.

One solution that really seems to work is called "Five Things First." The idea is to do five small things first thing in the morning, before your day officially begins.

Choose simple tasks like picking up the clothes off the floor or putting dishes into the dishwasher. The key is to pick tasks that are easy to accomplish and that lighten the load of your non-ADHD partner. Just think how different your relationship could be if you accomplished 25 things before the weekend!

~ Sarah A. Ferman, L.M.F.T., P.C.C.
& Robert L. Wilford, Ph.D.

Sarah Ferman, L.M.F.T., P.C.C., & Robert Wilford, Ph.D., are leading ADHD Couples Consultants, helping ADHD Couples reconnect and create loving and enduring relationships. www.ADHDCouplesConsultants.com

The 7-Step PowerPlan to Success™
Step #7: Expect Backsliding

One of the most difficult things about ADD/ADHD is its inconsistency. Because you can do some things sometimes (maybe the sun and the moon are perfectly aligned), people don't understand why you can't do things consistently. What works today may not work tomorrow; just one more reason to have a large toolbox of strategies. Also a reason *not* to get down on yourself when things don't work the way you planned: the 7 steps are a circular process.

If you expect that for every two steps forward you'll take one step back, the backsliding doesn't disappoint you as much as if you had expected continual improvement or to even maintain status quo. Dieters who blow their diet have a choice: give up and continue to binge or accept it was a tough diet day, powerfully enjoy the food, then opt to get back on track.

~Susan Lasky, MA, BCC, SCAC

Susan Lasky, Master ADD/ADHD Strategist, Productivity Coach & Professional Organizer, creator of the 7-Step PowerPlan to Success™ and the 28-Day Accountability Challenge™. www.SusanLasky.com ~ www.PowerPlanToSuccess.com ~ Susan@SusanLasky.com

Surroundings Matter

Stop trying to swim upstream. In other words, work *with* your surroundings to help you do what you want or need to do.

- If you know you study better in the library than in the café, then go to the library.

- If you are more focused on work when you're in the office than when you are working from home then for goodness sake, go to the office.

- If you want to lose weight and you know that you eat more in front of the TV than at the table, then (DUH!) eat at the table.

- If you want to exercise but that stationary bike hasn't been ridden since the week after you brought it home, get rid of the bike, save the space, and go to the gym. Pay attention to what helps you do what you want and need to do. Use that knowledge to get things done.

~Sarah D. Wright, M.S., A.C.T.

Nationally-known ADHD coach Sarah D. Wright specializes in helping professionals in small businesses get on track and get going. FocusForEffectiveness.com ~ Sarah@FocusForEffectiveness.com (858) 408-9338.

Think Like Leonardo da Vinci

For years I have been using a process called mind mapping. I love how it helps get the best ideas out of your brain and onto paper or screen. It's exceptionally well suited for those with ADHD, allowing us to free up our creativity while still generating ideas in an organized fashion. The key to mind mapping is that it gives your brain free rein to capture any thought that comes to mind, and associates that thought with your other ideas. It is far superior to outlining, which forces you to organize thoughts while you generate them.

Mind mapping traces back to Leonardo da Vinci. He used it throughout his notebooks, literally recording his thoughts moment by moment. Today, there are numerous software programs available that can help you. Google "mind-mapping" and check them out. Think like da Vinci!

~Paul O'Connor, MCC

Paul O'Connor coaches business executives with ADHD. He is a Master Certified Coach, secretary of the Professional Association of ADHD Coaches, based in Atlanta. (404) 377-4712 paul@EnergyForLifeCoach.com ~ www.EnergyForLifeCoach.com

Play Your Chores (All the World's a Game)

All it takes is a little creativity. It can be exhausting, but think of it as energy saved not having to cajole people to get their chores done. Bottom line: If you can make it a game, do it! There is no age limit on this advice (i.e. it works for spouses, too).

People with ADHD are motivated by:

1. Novelty

2. Competition

3. Urgency

4. Interest

Seriously, it's a lot more fun to throw dirty socks through a hoop than into a laundry basket. And what about singing into a wooden spoon while unloading the dishwasher - MUCH more fun than just putting stuff away! Use this to your advantage and PLAY your chores away!

~ *Elaine Taylor-Klaus, CPCC, ACC, and Diane Dempster, MHSA, CPC, ACC*

ImpactADHD helps parents help kids. Elaine Taylor-Klaus & Diane Dempster provide reality-based training, with coaching to make it stick. We help your family thrive! http://www.ImpactADHD.com

How to Get Up in the Morning

D you struggle to get up and out of bed in the morning? Here are a few tips to get you moving: Drink a quart of water before bed (you'll have to get up to go pee).

- Sleep with your dog in your room and the door closed (you'll have to get up to let the dog go pee).
- Use two alarm clocks; take your meds at the first alarm, and get out of bed at the second.
- Put your second alarm clock where it will make someone else really mad if it goes off.
- Get a rolling alarm clock that rolls away so you have to chase it to turn it off.
- Get a really loud alarm clock with a bed shaker attachment (check out www.sonicalert.com).
- Have an agreement with someone to pull your covers off and pour water on you if you don't get up on time!

~Sarah D. Wright, M.S., A.C.T.

Nationally-known ADHD coach Sarah D. Wright specializes in helping professionals in small businesses get on track and get going. FocusForEffectiveness.com ~ Sarah@FocusForEffectiveness.com (858) 408-9338.

"If you want to have something in your life you have never had, you have to do something in your life you have never done."

~ JD Houston

Feed Your Unique ADD/ADHD Brain

The ADDer has unique dietary needs that, if ignored, magnify our ADHD. Here are 4 cardinal ADD diet rules:

1) **Sugar Sucks:** it gives you a mental jolt but quickly dissipates, leaving you in the gutter jonesing for more. You can't have your cake and eat it too.

2) **Carbs Kill:** they turn into sugar, and we already know sugar sucks. Not all carbs are created equal; complex carbs, like whole grain breads/cereal, brown rice, yams, veggies, seeds and nuts, are okay. Steer clear of simple carbs, a.k.a. "white foods."

3) **Protein is Power:** it triggers neurotransmitters that help us focus. Get quality protein in fish, beans, dairy and protein drinks/powders (that aren't loaded with sugar!).

4) **Omegas are Mega:** Omega-3s/-6s improve brain function. Get more with fish or krill oil supplements. Get omegas and protein via walnuts, pistachios, pine nuts and sardines.

~Alan Brown

Alan Brown, a struggling exec until diagnosed with ADD, crafted the success strategies in ADD Crusher™ videos: interactive tools helping ADDers live to their potential. www.ADDCrusher.com

A Tip We Need, Yet Rarely Heed (WARNING: This is a Word Game)

Here is a Suggestion that we've all heard before. The fact that we read and hear about this tip Frequently is a good indication of its importance.

Yet, most ADD-ers, *including me*, do not usually follow this advice as we busily take care of the many Responsibilities that fill Our day. The challenge in heeding this particular advice further points to the fundamental Level at which the change needs to be made. This is not a new strategy, rather a 'reminder tip' for Each of Us. Can you guess what it is?

Unscramble the **eight (8) bolded CAPITAL** letters above to form the missing word:

PUT _ _ _ _ _ _ _ _ FIRST
(see answer below author bio)

~Monika Pompetzki, ADHD Coach

Monika Pompetzki, BSc, MEd, AD/HD, academic, & life coach focused on enjoying puzzles & games, especially those of everyday life. www.add-adhdCoaching.com ~ monika@add-adhdCoaching.com ~ (905) 336-8330 (answer: YOURSELF)

Now is Not the Time

I prioritize my activities well, but I'm also easily distracted. So, when I leave my office to do a specific task, I find myself surrounded by "distraction minefields:" that pile of things I need to file, an unfinished project, the morning paper. Each has the potential to keep me from doing what I intended to do.

To combat those distractions, I memorized the phrase, "Now is not the time." I repeated that line over and over again until it stuck. When I hear that little voice now, it's like a warning signal. It tells me I'm about to get into something I didn't originally intend to do. It helps me pause long enough to realize that now isn't the time to do that activity that just caught my attention. It's just a distraction. There will be another time for that project to get done. Now is the time to focus on my main task.

~Paul O'Connor, MCC

Paul O'Connor coaches business executives with ADHD. He is a Master Certified Coach, secretary of the Professional Association of ADHD Coaches, based in Atlanta. (404) 377-4712 paul@EnergyForLifeCoach.com ~ www.EnergyForLifeCoach.com

HELLO? HELLO? Did You Hear Anything I Said?

The ADHD brain can be very difficult for a non-ADHD partner to understand. As you jump from thought to thought, your partner can be left at point K, when you have already reached point Z.

Learn to validate your spouse's feelings and thoughts. Sit across from each other to talk and use "I feel" statements, focusing on how you feel instead of starting with "You..." and speaking at or for your partner. Avoid words like "never" and "always." Remember to give positive feedback. Respect and understand your partner's perspective; clarify and check out assumptions, which are often misinterpretations. All humans have a deep need to feel understood, connected and appreciated. Don't leave your partner in the dust as your brain cruises the Autobahn; instead, focus on slowing down, speaking directly to each other and finding common ground.

~Sherry Clarke, MA, LCMFT

Sherry Clarke, MA, LCMFT, a veteran Licensed Marriage and Family Therapist and ADHD Coach, has a passion for helping couples and parents understand, embrace and celebrate their ADHD. www.clarkecoaching.com

Summertime Blues

Summertime is supposed to be when the livin' is easy. Our days are longer, life is more carefree and we can relax and move at a slower pace. How can those warm months cause anything but happiness?

As seasons change, so do many of our routines that we so diligently adhered to during the other times of the year, including bedtime rituals, eating habits and exercise regimes. The problem is that whenever our routine changes, external structures can begin to crumble and we may not even be aware of it until we notice those dreaded feelings of unproductively, chaos and overwhelm.

Awareness is key. Simply be aware that during certain times of the year, such as summer and holidays, those structures and routines are more susceptible to slipping away. If we are aware, we can create new routines and structures so that we will only see blue skies!

~Laurie Dupar, ADHD Coach & Expert

Laurie Dupar, PMHNP, RN, PCC, is an internationally-recognized ADHD expert. She is the editor of *365+1 ways to succeed with ADHD*. www.coachingforadhd.com ~ (916) 791-1799

Knowledge is Power

You can learn to hold your head high, even in a sea of put-downs. Take time and get to know the real you and your potential. Start with the person deep inside of you. Listen to that calm voice speak of dreams, desires, and aspirations. Then realize how your ADHD affects you. You can't avoid obstacles until you recognize how they detour you. Set a path to building a team from the people who care about you. Let this team guide you from a simple path to the wider road that will lead to many successes.

~Dulce Torres, LPC-S, BCC, ADHD Coach

Dulce Torres, Licensed Professional Counselor, Board Certified Coach, specializes in ADHD coaching that helps teenagers, adults, and parents to find their hidden strengths. http://www.dstcoaching.com ~ dtorres@dstcoaching.com

Couples & ADHD: Jump-Start Your Mornings Together

Mornings are often a major challenge for people with ADHD as medications can take an hour to kick in. Why not greet your partner fully medicated? You will need:

1 shot glass

1 bottle of water

An alarm clock with 2 alarm settings

Medication

Here's how it works: Put your bottled water and shot glass (which don't tip over easily) on your nightstand. Place your medications into the shot glass. Now, set alarm #1 to go off one hour before you want to get up. Set alarm #2 for your actual "get out of bed" time. When alarm #1 goes off, take your medications and go back to sleep. When alarm #2 goes off, you'll be ready to get up out of bed. You'll be clear and motivated to greet your partner with medications in place.

~ Sarah A. Ferman, L.M.F.T., P.C.C.
& Robert L. Wilford, Ph.D.

Sarah Ferman, L.M.F.T., P.C.C., & Robert Wilford, Ph.D., are leading ADHD Couples Consultants, helping ADHD Couples reconnect and create loving and enduring relationships. www.ADHDCouplesConsultants.com

Caution! Be Nice to Yourself!

It is important to settle the load limit before it explodes and causes you to do something that you regret! For instance, if you don't feed yourself on time, you might impulsively attack that food you regret. It is just the same with working or studying. When I force myself into doing something too long, my frustration is big. If I ignore breaks and rewards for myself, at the end the load limit goes off, which leads me to take a couple of breaks at once and then I get disconnected! Here is what I try to do:

- I try to exercise in the mornings, as this alleviates my fidgets.
- I reward myself by making an e-puzzle on my iPad or playing Angry Birds. It is also efficient when you shift your attention from one task to another! I like myself better when I'm kind and gentle with myself.

~Eda Aydogan, MA, ACC, PACG

Eda Aydogan, MA, ACC, PACG, ADHD Coach, specializes in helping you understand your own ADHD and find coping strategies. For more information, find me at www.dehbka.com. eaydogan@dehbka.com

Jumping is Okay - for Johnny and Sally!

ADHD kids have lots of energy and need to have a safe place to release it - *not* on your white living room couch! Purchase a child-sized, in-home, mini trampoline (rebounder), choose a safe corner to set it up, and then encourage them to jump often throughout the day. The jumping reduces hyperactivity and "lights" up the brain. It promotes healthy bodies, too, by exercising all the cells and the immune system. I bought one for two of my grandsons; they love it and so do their parents! The boys say, "Going to get my energy out, Mommy!" A child's bouncing ball with a handle or a jump rope are good alternatives. The key is to acknowledge that your children's ADHD bodies want and need to jump. Make it be a safe and frequent activity for them!

~Sherry Clarke, MA, LCMFT, ACG

Sherry Clarke, MA, LCMFT, a veteran Licensed Marriage and Family Therapist and ADHD Coach, has a passion for helping couples and parents understand, embrace and celebrate their ADHD. www.clarkecoaching.com

One Gas Burner at a Time

Ever had the experience of trying to cook too many dishes at once and you end up ruining all of them? When you cook several dishes simultaneously, you have to adjust the temperature on one burner, stir the pot on the second, add ingredients to one dish, or take the lid off another. Juggling too many tasks like this can cause one pot to boil over or another to burn. Our brains are similar to a busy kitchen. If you free your mind to focus on preparing just one dish really well, you can take your time, enjoy the process and get fabulous results. This approach applies to many areas in your life; it's better to prioritize and cross off one task or goal at a time so you won't overwhelm your brain. These smaller victories will send your adrenaline pumping and boost your motivation to move onto the next task.

~Dr. Billi

The AttentionB Method, Pedagogical/Class Management for ADHD with Dr. Billi, Ph.D. Tame the chaos in your classroom using my unique strategies. www.AttentionB.com ~ DrBilli@AttentionB.com ~ (855) DrBilli

Use Less Words

ADHD can be called an information-processing disorder: not enough neurotransmitters are working properly to synthesis the information pouring into the brain. Too much information can cause overload, which stops the brain. It is for this reason that children often miss the direction they are given. As parents, we often think, *If I explain it in a different way this time, or tell him what type of problems it creates when he doesn't do what he is told, I am sure he will understand this time.*

In fact, increasing the complexity of the direction by using more words will confuse your child more. When giving direction to your child, use less words and you will enable him to better process the information you are giving him.

~Judith Champion, MSW, ACG

Judith Champion, MSW, ACG, ADHD Family Coach and Educator, ADHD Associates, mother and grandmother to ADHD adults and children. www.ADHDAssociates.com ~ judith@judithchampion.com ~ (609) 468-0819

Bright Shiny Coach Syndrome©

ADHD coaching is fast being recognized as a key in experiencing long-lasting success with ADHD. Sometimes it is easy to get distracted by prices or get swept up in another's credentials. Choosing the right coach for you or your child is important. Here are some questions to consider before deciding on the best coach for you:

- What are their certifications/credentials in coaching?
- Where/how did they get their ADHD expertise?
- What is this coach's specialty (parenting, college, child)? Does it match your needs?
- How will this coach monitor my progress?
- What are the sessions like?
- Do they work in person, over the phone, or using Skype? Does this work for me?

Finally, the "gut response" question: "Do I <u>want</u> to work with this coach?" Coaching is a partnership, and feeling like you connect with your coach and that they "get" you may be the tie breaker.

~Laurie Dupar, ADHD Coach & Expert

Laurie Dupar is an internationally-recognized expert, coach, author and speaker on ADHD and coaching. You can reach her at <u>www.coachingforadhd.com</u> or (916) 791-1799.

5 Steps to Re-Boot Productivity After an Emotional Crash

Negativity is like a nasty computer virus, hijacking your motivation and bogging down your system until you "crash." Guilt, embarrassment and shame often trigger procrastination, like when you put off that dentist appointment because you haven't flossed. Here are 5 steps to re-motivate yourself:

1. Do the least upsetting aspect of a task first: If sorting bills creates guilt, *only* open the envelopes. Sort them into piles by month later. No peeking!

2. Delegate highly emotional tasks to others: For example, put the payment to your ex-spouse on auto bill pay.

3. Connect distasteful tasks with positive payoffs: Make a list of what you'll get out of filing those taxes.

4. Protect your positivity: Invite a buddy over or play music that uplifts you.

5. Hold yourself accountable: Find an accountability group, support and more at www.adhdpower.com/productivity.

~Sunny Aldrich, Professional ADHD Coach

Sunny Aldrich is the first professional ADHD Coach in Alaska. She specializes in emotional procrastination, ADHD strength assessment, dyslexia, and homeschooling. http://www.adhdpower.com ~ sunny@adhdpower.com.

The ONE Factor That Keeps You Stuck: Blame

One factor that keeps people stuck: BLAME. So, how do we let it go? Break through with these three steps:

1) Listen. Be sure to listen with a filter. Some things won't serve you. If you get offended by someone, then that's where you should pay the most attention. The offense is always within.

2) Take Responsibility. It's not about the bad job or the lousy break you got. It's about what you do with those things. How you respond, own, and use them. Getting responsible means getting results.

3) Care Less. Feelings. Opinions. Results. Spend time getting clear on what you care about and what you could care less about.

You can have all the money and success in the world, but if you choose to blame other people or things, you will always be a hostage. Set yourself free.

~Suzanne Evans, CEO

Suzanne Evans is the founder of Suzanne Evans Coaching, LLC, ranked #225 in Inc 500 for 2012. She supports, coaches, and teaches over 30,000 women enrolled in her wealth and business-building programs.

A Job Worth Doing is Worth Doing BADLY, too!

Many ADDers struggle with black-and-white thinking (a.k.a. perfectionism). While doing the very best you can is laudable, that desire sometimes leads to rumination and inaction. The answer is to lower your standards! Nobody has time to do everything perfectly. "Good enough" is often fine. Any shade of completion beats chronic indecision and procrastination.

Try the "Least and Quickest" game when you're stuck: "What's the *least* I can do to get this done and the *quickest* way I can get it off my plate?" Aspiring to a "C-" job reduces pressure, anxiety and rumination. Forget about doing it "right;" get it *done*! When you're shooting for straight A's on everything, where do you think you get the time for an A+ job on what's important to *you*? Play "least and quickest" with everything for one week. You'll not only get more done, you'll be clearer on where you should focus your A+ energy.

~Madelyn Griffith-Haynie, CTP, CMC, A.C.T., MCC, SCAC

Madelyn Griffith-Haynie, multi-certified Lifecoach pioneer; founder of The Optimal Functioning Institute™, the earth's first ADD-specific coach training program; and co-founder of the ADD coaching field. mgh@addcoach.com ~ www.ADDandSoMuchMore.com

No More Wash-Day Blues

Younger folks say how difficult it is to get the washing done. I remember when I was young, with a family of grubby boys, how it was a painful, never-ending chore. Now, as an elder ADDer, laundry is a cinch. I do a small load every day; it's easier than brushing my teeth! Five minutes to transfer the wet things to the dryer, (or hang them on the line in summer) and later they go to a basket near my lazy chair, where I fold as I watch TV. There is always a washing in the works, but nothing accumulates. Putting away is the hardest part, but it does get done - usually when I am looking for my favorite jeans. Making laundry a daily chore, in small stages, works for me. PS: I haven't owned an iron for over 50 years!

~Jane Patrick, BA, MEd.

Jane Patrick, retired teacher, diagnosed with ADD at age 75. Now enjoying the trip! Advocate for neglected group of 60+ ADDers.
janeham@abacom.com

Plan C

When you have an idea or plan in your head, it HAS to happen that way, right? We often hold fast to our perfectly devised or intended Plan A. But life doesn't always go that way, does it? Often, we have to resort to Plan B. But frankly, my brain doesn't want to do Plan B! Does yours?

What to do? Skip Plan B and use your creativity to formulate Plan C (that's C for create!).

When your Plan A has been foiled, instead of blowing up or freaking out, start asking, "What parts of the original plan could still be used? What can I now consider in the new circumstance?"

Allow Plan C to unfold in your life. Giving Plan C your attention and energy, it could be just the Plan A you were hoping for and maybe even better!

~Melissa Fahrney, M.A., CPC

Melissa Fahrney, certified ADHD Coach & School Psychologist in Montana, specializes in heart-centered coaching for young people.... "Master your Mountain with Heart." 1coachmelissa@gmail.com ~ www.addheartworks.com

Summary: The 7-Step PowerPlan to Success™ with ADHD!

Step 1: Be aware of your strengths and challenges, likes and dislikes, and what you are doing (or not).

Step 2: Accept that this is where you are and who you are at this time, without judgment.

Step 3: Realize that you have the power of choice. Possibility exists, and you can choose to transform your life.

Step 4: Clarify what you want to change, determine specific objectives and prioritize your goals.

Step 5: Learn targeted strategies that will jumpstart your brain and help change existing patterns.

Step 6: Begin taking action, even baby steps, toward achieving those goals.

Step 7: Expect backsliding, even failures, but keep going. Cultivate self-awareness, acceptance and the belief in possibility that will keep you moving forward. If needed, re-examine and edit your goals and priorities. Take charge of your life!

~Susan Lasky, MA, BCC, SCAC

Susan Lasky, Master ADD/ADHD Strategist, Productivity Coach & Professional Organizer, creator of the 7-Step PowerPlan to Success™ and the 28-Day Accountability Challenge™. www.SusanLasky.com ~ www.PowerPlanToSuccess.com ~ Susan@SusanLasky.com

"Knowing is not enough; we must apply. Willing is not enough; we must do."

~ Goethe

"Free Time Wish Bowl"

Remember driving by a restaurant and thinking, "Hmmm I'd like to go there one day?" Do you have a book that you wish to read or a movie to watch? Do you wish to have a guilt-free day to stay in bed, watch TV or do whatever you desire? Then, when you finally have that free time, suddenly you no longer remember all those places you'd like to try or things you want to do?

With life so busy, our wishes may get lost in the hustle and bustle of daily tasks. A "Free Time Wish Bowl" is a fun and easy way to remember your someday wishes.

Write your wish on an index card or piece of paper and place it in a decorative bowl. During one of these free times when you're pondering on what to do, reach in the bowl, select a card and follow your wish.

~Cindy Giardina, PCC

Cindy Giardina, Professional Certified Coach helping adults and students take charge of their ADHD. cindy@kaleidoscope-coaching.com ~ (973) 694-5077

"Note" the Time

Because many people with ADHD seem to do better when things are within their line of sight, having visual reminders of what needs to be done (and when) can be very helpful. For one teen who had particular difficulty getting to school on time, post it notes shaped as arrows were placed directly on the outside frame of analog clocks in his bathroom, bedroom or kitchen pointing to the time particular tasks needed to be done.

With reminders for "Start your shower," "Go get dressed," "Go downstairs to eat," or "Leave for school" on the clocks in his environment, he didn't lose track of time and was able to keep to his morning schedule. The added bonus for his parents was that if he wasn't on track, his parents didn't need to nag, but only needed to remind him to look at the clocks.

For more ideas, visit www.FocusForEffectiveness.com/blog.

~Roxanne Fouche, ADHD Coach

Roxanne Fouche, ADHD Coach, helps both students and women live successfully with ADHD and related challenges. In person, phone, or Skype. Contact (858) 484-4749 or Roxanne@FocusForEffectiveness.com.

Become Best Friends with Your Smartphone

U se your calendar and reminder apps on your Smartphone. Set a reminder alarm 15, 30 or even 60 minutes before any appointment to help you be on time for your appointment. Make sure that you set as many multiple alarms as you need up until the time of the appointment to ensure that you will be on time. You can also schedule in free time, time to complete certain tasks, meals, reminders to call someone, etc. You may want to experiment with different alarm sounds for different types of activities. Technology can be your friend.

~ Alan R. Graham, Ph.D., PCC, SCAC

Alan R. Graham, Ph.D., PCC, SCAC, trains ADD coaches for Mentorcoach, coaches executives with business and organizational challenges, and works with ADHD adults, teens, children and parents. www.ADDvisor.com ~ (847) 824-1235

Say Again?

ADHD can get in the way of someone's paying attention to, understanding, and/or remembering what someone else is saying. When kids are small, parents often get their children's attention before they speak and then ask them to repeat back what was understood. As we get older, it's up to us to practice good listening skills with family, friends, teachers and people at work. We need to let someone else finish speaking before we say something. (Not an easy task for many of us!) We can also ask questions to make sure we understand and remember what was said. It could be as simple as asking for repetition: "I'm sorry, can you repeat that?"; asking clarifying questions: "So is the meeting at 10:00 or 10:30 on Tuesday?"; or, confirming your understanding: "Okay, just so we're on the same page, you want me to have this ready by the 14th?"

~Roxanne Fouche, ADHD Coach

Roxanne Fouche, ADHD Coach, helps both students and women live successfully with ADHD and related challenges. In person, phone, or Skype. Contact (858) 484-4749 or Roxanne@FocusForEffectiveness.com.

Gift or Disability: Positive Focus Assures Success

Attention deficit is a blessing. If you focus solely on the negative, you assure negative outcomes. As a parent of ADHD children, I regret wasting so much energy on spirit-defeating deficits, trying to beat square pegs into round holes. Henry Ford said, "Whether you think you can or think you can't - you're right." Those who succeed with ADHD focus intently on their strengths. They work around their deficits, whether by collaborating with those who have complementary skills (such as coaches, significant others, and employees) or avoiding certain types of work. When focused intently on your passions and natural gifts and freed from the burden of your deficits, the sky is truly the limit. As Albert Einstein once said, "Everybody is a genius. But if you judge a fish by its ability to climb a tree, it will live its whole life believing that it is stupid."

~Susan S. Wilder, MD, CEO

Susan Wilder, MD, is an innovative Family Physician with expertise in advanced nutritional interventions for mood and attention disorders. Visit www.lifescapearizona.com or follow on Facebook: https://www.facebook.com/LifeScapePremier.

Always Start With What is Going on in Your Mind

ADHD people have a hard time doing the right thing at the right time. They only work when there is an interest. My problem is concentrating when my mind is in a completely different place. When I prepare for a project, I allow myself some time beforehand. I use this time to focus on what I need to do. I create a mind map. I put "Tana's mind" at the core. I write about my thoughts and feelings at that moment, and why I feel that way. Although these thoughts could be completely out of context, I let them come. I pause and ask myself, what else? After I deplete my thoughts and clear my mind, the project appears. I then write about my thoughts and feelings about the project. The last action is determining a small step to start . By acting on that step, I have already started!

~Suzan Tana Alalu, MA, ACC, PACG

Suzan Tana Alalu, MA in Psychology and Expressive Arts, ACC, Professional ADHD Coach in Turkey, specializes in transforming your attention and relationship systems. talalu@dehbka.com

When it Won't Stick in Your Head, Stick it Somewhere Else

Write hard-to-remember information on an index card, then leave the card where the information is needed. Can't remember which buttons switch the sound system from TV output to iPod output? Tape instructions to the side of the stereo. Do you need to use a special cleanser on your countertops? Name it, then tape it to the inside of the cabinet door where you keep your cleaning supplies. Sometimes forget how many scoops of coffee to put in the coffee maker? Put the card where you keep the coffee and filters.

Index cards can be placed just about anywhere, and you can cut them into smaller sizes if needed.

Added Bonus: This method makes it easier for visiting house guests to help themselves.

~Terri Gantt, ADHD Coach

Terri Gantt, ADHD Coach, helps adults develop realistic strategies to overcome challenges, leverage abilities and achieve the results they desire. Check us out: www.UpstateADHDCoaching.com. Terri@UpstateADHDCoaching.com.

Managing ADHD with Diet

The correlation between diet and ADHD is often overlooked. Some crucial points to remember: Eat a well-balanced diet based on whole, natural foods. Focus on combining healthy fats, proteins and complex carbohydrates (primarily vegetables). Reducing simple carbohydrates and sugary foods while eating enough healthy fats and proteins will minimize blood sugar spikes and drops, which can lead to brain fog, memory loss, and mood swings. The more meals and snacks you prepare yourself, using fresh or frozen ingredients, the less you will come in contact with additives that may trigger ADHD reactions. These include: any food dyes with a number ("Yellow No. 5," "Red 40," "Blue #1," etc.), corn syrup, high fructose corn syrup, and artificial sweeteners (except Stevia). Avoid foods listing "natural flavors" as an ingredient; many of these are created in labs, far from natural, and can be extremely reactive.

~Jennifer Beck, Registered Nutrition Consultant & Corporate Health Coach

Jennifer Beck, Registered Nutrition Consultant, teaches clients a wellness-based approach to ADHD treatment that maximizes concentration without reliance upon prescription drugs. www.AdvancedWellnessCoaching.com ~ (513) 407-5775

Focus on the Whole

No one is just a person with ADHD, even if it sometimes feels that way. For example, I am female, a daughter, a Midwestern farm girl, a sister, a teacher, a mentor, an avid reader, a lesbian, an inattentive ADDer, and a cat guardian. Each of those labels represents a part of me, but it takes all of them and many more to define me. We are each a very unique combination of genetics, brain wiring, experience, culture, values, and personal choices. The world needs each of us in all our unique diversity. Let's not strive for some illusive (and probably boring) "normal" when we can be living from and celebrating our uniqueness. As Professor Dumbledore said, "It is our choices, Harry, that show what we truly are, far more than our abilities." What do you love to do? What are you naturally good at doing? Choose passion and enjoy your life.

~Barbara Luther, Master Certified Coach

Barbara Luther, President, Professional Association of ADHD Coaches, www.PAACCoaches.org. Director of Training, ADD Coach Academy, www.addca.com. Master Certified ADHD Coach. www.WindBeneathYourWings.com ~ www.SoaringCoachesCircle.com St. Louis, MO ~ 573-340-3559

ADHD and Family Business

When one or more members of the family have ADHD and they also run a family business, life can get extremely complicated. I suggest that, as much as possible, the role of parent-child be overlooked. Professionally, family members must assume the roles of employer-employee.

In addition, providing structure and job descriptions with concrete and specific duties are helpful in minimizing misunderstandings. Arguments between family members should be avoided in the workplace as much as possible. If disagreements do arise, however, make sure to discuss them in a private location away from other employees.

I suggest that, when issues do arise among the family members, somebody who is trusted by the owners is asked to act as a buffer between them to help them resolve the issue. Remember that you are acting as a role model for your employees!

~Roya Kravetz, ADHD and Business Coach

Roya Kravetz is a Credentialed Life Coach who specializes in ADHD Coaching. She is also a Certified Executive Coach who helps professionals with ADHD. www.adhdsuccesscoaching.com

My Job Review Sucks!

Situation: My job reviews are really bad and agonizing. I can't think of anything good to say; all I remember is what I didn't do. Then I feel foolish, remembering everything after the review is over.

Strategy: Most office desks have a pull-out drawer that holds hanging files. Create a file labeled "review." Place it in the front of the drawer. Every time you get an attaboy/girl, print it off and toss it in the file. If after a meeting someone says "great job on . . .", write a note for the file. Did an email come in with the status of a project - a deadline accomplished? Did you go out of your way to help someone, jeopardizing your time to complete your project? Write it down with the time spent and put it in the file. Writing that review will become much easier.

~Joyce Kubik, ADHD Coach, CC (IAC)

Joyce Kubik, Certified Life and ADHD Coach for students and adults, author of planning journals developed specifically for ADHD. Find it and more at www.bridgetosuccess.net.

Getting Your Child to...Take a Shower?

Following directions: what seems simple is actually complex. If your child is watching TV and you want him/her to take a shower, there are many steps involved for your child:

1. Notice: there is something else going on besides TV
2. Decide: Mom's voice is more important than TV
3. Stop: focusing on TV
4. Focus: on Mom's voice
5. Listen: for the details
6. Avoid: going back to TV
7. Determine: what Mom wants
8. Take action: by hitting the shower
9. Complete: the follow-through

While these are not all the steps, you get the picture. Bottom line: Your child doesn't really hear what you are asking. What's the solution? Get your child's attention first! First, say their name, then make eye contact and finally make your request.

~Elaine Taylor-Klaus, CPCC, ACC & Diane Dempster, MHSA, CPC, ACC

ImpactADHD helps parents help kids. Elaine Taylor-Klaus & Diane Dempster provide reality-based training, with coaching to make it stick. We help your family thrive! http://www.ImpactADHD.com

Shift to the Positive

I t is easy to get caught up in the negative aspects of the challenges that ADD presents. Keep in mind, however, that there are many positive ways to put your ADD tendencies to work for you, and the first step is to simply to shift your way of thinking about them. What a difference it can make to stop seeing yourself as "unpredictable," for example, and instead see yourself as "creative." The words we use to describe our behaviors range along a spectrum from less to more desirable. So, what would it take to turn "restless" into "eager"? "Impatient" into "energetic"? "Chatty" into "collaborative"? "Intense" into "focused"? "Aggressive" into "assertive"? "Anxious" into "cautious"? "Controlling" into "determined"? By changing the way you think about your own tendencies, you are on your way to becoming someone defined primarily by your positive attributes—someone who has a great deal to offer in almost any situation.

~Christina Fabrey, MEd, BCC, ACAC

Christina Fabrey is a certified Life and ADHD Coach specializing in transition to college and college students. www.vtcoaching.com ~ cfabrey@gmail.com ~ (802) 345-2046

You Are Smart AND You Have ADHD

How can someone be "smart," have graduated from college, tested as gifted, get decent grades in school and still have ADHD? It is a mistaken belief that someone who graduates from college cannot have ADHD. In fact, many people with ADHD are talented and intelligent, but due to the problems of inattention, distractibility, poor time management, disorganization or impulsivity, they do not achieve their fullest potential.

Each person experiences ADHD in a slightly different way. For some, the symptoms are mild and their strengths help them compensate. For others, their challenges in some areas of ADHD are severe, and they have not found ways to compensate yet in a successful way. Some of the most gifted and intelligent people were/are ADHD. Albert Einstein, Walt Disney, Winston Churchill and Thomas Edison all had ADHD, and look how they turned out!

~Laurie Dupar, PMHNP, RN, PCC Certified ADHD Coach and Nurse Practitioner

Laurie Dupar, PMHNP, RN, PCC, is a trained psychiatric mental health nurse practitioner and certified ADHD coach. You can find out more at www.coachingforadhd.com.

How Do You Eat an Elephant?

A re you so overwhelmed with all the things you want to change in your life (organize that closet, file those papers, make those calls, paint the kitchen, exercise, lose weight) that you can't get started on any of it? Remember the joke, "How do you eat an elephant? One bite at a time!" This applies to life, too. We can accomplish those things, but only one bit at a time. Break up goals or projects into smaller pieces. Do just one new thing for a week, then add another, then another, and so on. As one client observed, "It helped me to understand that although the changes I want in my life are major, those major changes can always be broken down into smaller components. When the components are smaller, they're not so overwhelming."

~Sarah D. Wright, M.S., A.C.T.

Nationally-known ADHD coach Sarah D. Wright specializes in helping professionals in small businesses get on track and get going. FocusForEffectiveness.com ~ Sarah@FocusForEffectiveness.com ~ 858-408-9338

Workstations Help You Get Things Done

Do you get derailed on tasks because you can't find something you need? Do you find that you go looking for that missing piece, get distracted, and don't get back to what you were doing? Make it easier. Create workstations that have everything you need:

- For sorting mail: within arm's reach, put both a trash/recycling bin and a place to put the sorted mail for different people in your household.

- For paying bills: you'll need either a computer for online payment or a "work kit" that contains bills to be paid, checks, envelopes, stamps, and pens. Put your work kit close to the place where you'll file the paperwork you plan to keep and a trash/shredding bin for discarded items.

- For scheduling: gather a master calendar, a message board, a place to keep incoming written notes and announcements, important phone numbers, pencils, pens, sticky notes, etc.

~Sarah D. Wright, M.S., A.C.T.

Nationally-known ADHD coach Sarah D. Wright specializes in helping professionals in small businesses get on track and get going. FocusForEffectiveness.com ~ Sarah@FocusForEffectiveness.com ~ 858-408-9338

Focus on Your Strengths

Empower others to be your best teammate by taking over your weak points.

Fuel your vision.

Be, do, and have what you love and are best at.

Such high vibrational energy of joy and high self-esteem empowers mastery and allows you to share your strengths with others on your team. This creates a win-win situation - and strategy - for everyone.

~Nancy Anne Brighton, LCSW, ADHD Coach

Nancy Anne Brighton, LCSW, ADHD Coach, empowers gifted adults with upside-down brilliance to create compelling futures from the future. Bright Brains Building. Brighter Future. www.BrightONBrains.com ~ ADHDcoach@BrightonBrains.com ~ (386) 290-6703

Getting More Things Done - Pomodoro Style

Staying on task can challenge even the most disciplined person. One of the best methods I have found for getting things done is called the Pomodoro Technique.

It's simple, really. Get a timer and 3 sheets of paper. On sheet one write how much time you have to devote to tasks today, including time for phone calls, laundry, etc. Divide that time into "Pomodoros" (25-minute segments). Segment the work you need to accomplish into the Pomodoros (some tasks may take more than one).

Set your timer for 25 minutes and start to work. Write any distractions or new to-do's on sheet two for later on. After each Pomodoro take a 5-minute break, after 3 take a 30-minute break. For more details on The Pomodoro Technique visit http://www.ptscoaching.com/articles/the-pomodoro-technique/.

~Cindy Goldrich, Ed. M., ACA

Cindy Goldrich, Ed. M., ACA, Certified ADHD Parent & Teen Coach
www.PTScoaching.com~Cindy@PTScoaching.com~(516) 802-0593
Coaching available in New York and via telephone

Make a Truce with Time

The best way to fix time troubles? By keeping track of how much time we spend, just like we keep track of our money! How? Grab some colored markers and post-it notes, a sketch book, or travel log. Use whatever appeals to you! Make a bet with yourself to try it for one day *only*. *If you can keep track of *one day*, then try day two. If you can make it seven days in a row, give yourself a reward! Why? Because you are on your way to creating a habit! You can use the calendar on your phone or desktop, and give the reminders cool ring tones! The trick is to create a system that you like and will use. The goal: to be able to correctly estimate the amount of time a task will take to fully complete. This will help improve your time management skills!

~Sandy Alletto Corbin, MA, ACG, SCAC

Sandy Alletto Corbin, a Senior Credentialed ADHD Coach and teacher, woman with ADHD and a single mother of an ADHD daughter, specializes in coaching women, teens and college students and advocating for change. www.lifecoachsandyalletto.com

Make a Challenge Out Of It

One concept I frequently use with clients when they are struggling to change something is to make a "challenge" out of it. Games like this are great for those with ADHD. A challenge creates renewed interest for the brain and helps people to look at problems in a new way.

For example, if someone wastes a lot of time in chat rooms and wants to change that behavior, we might start by setting them up with a challenge to not enter any chat rooms for 7 days. We're not trying to eliminate the behavior all at once, just for 7 days.

Most people can successfully complete a 7-day challenge. I often move to 14-day or 30-day challenges as well, and have the person create a reward that's especially appealing to them. It's amazing how often the use of challenges and rewards eliminates long-term self-defeating behaviors.

~Paul O'Connor, MCC

Paul O'Connor coaches business executives with ADHD. He is a Master Certified Coach, secretary of the Professional Association of ADHD Coaches, based in Atlanta. (404) 377-4712 paul@EnergyForLifeCoach.com ~ www.EnergyForLifeCoach.com

The Queen of Denial...NOT!

When the doctor first suggested I had ADHD, I pictured a hyperactive little boy bouncing off the walls and knew that wasn't me. After seeing a few more doctors, I finally looked up information about adult ADHD. While reading it, I thought, "Holy cow, they're talking about me! How did they know that?" The biggest challenge I've had in dealing with ADHD is getting past denial. First, denial that I really had ADHD. Then denial of how much it truly impacted my life. I couldn't fix it myself and didn't ask for help because I was embarrassed to admit the problems I was having. But denying problems doesn't make them go away; it just makes them harder to deal with. Admitting problems is difficult and painful. But you can't fix something if you think it ain't broke. In acceptance, you find power to move forward in life and use your strengths to be successful.

~Rose Smith, M. Ed.

Rose Smith, M. Ed. For more helpful hints and random reflections, please visit http://RandomReflectionsbyRose.wordpress.com/.

The Power of Affirmation : I AM

Recently, I had a boss who was angry, depressed, judgmental, defensive about her lack of professional and personal development, rigid and demanding. She projected her self-loathing onto me and even yelled and belittled me like a bully. I started believing that I was worthless, and my behaviors and performance followed suit, until the point that her unbearable bullying lead to my resignation.

If you are not nurtured and empowered by your environment, leave now! You are responsible for who you truly are. Keep a recorder of your voice to play over and over to remind yourself who you are as a BEING. Never let anyone, including yourself, decree and project onto you any negative possibility of who you are creating yourself as a being. Create a life of your dreams now.

~Nancy Anne Brighton, LCSW, ADHD Coach

Nancy Anne Brighton, LCSW, ADHD Coach, empowers gifted adults with upside-down brilliance to create compelling futures from the future. Bright Brains Building. Brighter Future. www.BrightONBrains.com ~ ADHDcoach@BrightonBrains.com ~ (386) 290-6703

Bottom Up!

When clearing a pile of papers, rather than starting from the top and working your way down, do just the opposite - start from the bottom and work up. Put one hand on the top of the pile to steady it and pull items from the bottom. These are usually older, and often outdated and useless, making them easy to toss into the recycling/trash bin. Keep pulling from the bottom and when the first pile is done, start on the next one.

This is possibly the best tool I've ever come up with – I know from experience, it *always* works!

~Dee Shofner Doochin, MLAS, PCC, CMC, PACG, SCAC

Dee Shofner Doochin, MLAS; Professional Certified Coach; Certified Mentor Coach; Senior Certified ADHD Coach; wife, mother, grandmother, and great-grandmother with ADHD; adventurer; lover of life! www.deedoochin.com

It's Never Too Late

Are you over 60? Do you wonder why you are often late, forgetful, untidy, indecisive, unable to finish projects, and twirling in circles? Could it be ADD?

Consult someone who knows about elder adult ADD or is willing to listen to you, believe you, and think outside the box. There is still very little information about ADD in elders. Investigate the possibilities of medication and other types of treatment.

It was difficult, but I did find doctors and others who were able to help me. There is no longer a need to suffer. Make the last twenty or so years of your life the most contented and productive you've ever known! It's never too late. And to professionals: please document your cases of elder ADD, do research, publish, specialize, and make this a more recognizable disorder in older people.

~Jane Patrick, BA, MEd.

Jane Patrick, retired teacher, diagnosed with ADD at age 75. Now enjoying the trip! Advocate for neglected group of 60+ ADDers. janeham@abacom.com

"If you don't go after what you want, you'll never have it. If you don't ask, the answer is always no. If you don't step forward you're always in the same place."

~ Nora Roberts

Sleep time Disarmament Negotiations

Getting to sleep: big problem for many ADHDers. There are lots of good tips like block out **all** the light from your bedroom, switch off computer screens two hours before bedtime, tense and relax your muscles in turn, etc.

But the problem that's never mentioned is the fact that you have to **agree** with yourself that you will attempt to go to sleep now. It's as if the conscious bits of the brain simply don't want to switch themselves off. "I'll just let my body do this relaxation exercise while I carry on thinking all these lovely thoughts."

So I do a disarmament ceremony and make myself think: *I solemnly declare that I will do what it takes to go to sleep now. I will do nothing but my breathing exercises and think nothing but "in, 2, 3, 4, 5, out, 2, 3, 4, 5."* I breathe. In, 2, 3, 4, 5, etc. Sometimes sleep breaks out.

~Dr. Gillian Hayes, Ph.D.

Gillian Hayes, PhD, is an ADHD coach who specializes in helping students, academics and other high achievers dig out their best. gillian@brightshinycoaching.com

What Went Well?

As a parent and coach, I have noticed all the negativity in school, work and everyday life and its effects on my children and clients. As a coach, I ask each client, whether young, old, ADHD, Aspie or neurotypical, "What went well this week?" Borrowed from positive psychology, it starts our session celebrating successes and therefore sets a positive tone. No matter what kind of week they have had, they know I am going to ask, and they always find something that went well. For the younger clients, I have a *What Went Well* book where they can write in their successes. "What went well" works great with family members. Instead of asking "How was school/your day?" and getting a non-descriptive "Fine," they give greater details and share successes they can celebrate with you. Have them start their own *What Went Well* book and start focusing on what went right.

~Dana D. Maher, ADHD & Asperger's Life Coach

Dana D. Maher, Personal and Executive Life Coach for adolescents and adults, including those with Asperger's Syndrome and ADHD. ddmaher@yahoo.com ~ 908-377-8427

Barney Time

When my children were young, we did a lot of traveling by car. We drove long distances, sometimes driving 10 hours in a day!

I think spending this much time unplugged provided my kids a time to unwind, use their creativity, interact, make up games, color, read or entertain themselves. The most challenging part of these trips was that the kids were too young to be able to tell time by a clock and would constantly ask, "When we will get there?" To save our own sanity and help the kids have a sense of "how long," we began basing our trip distance on one of their popular TV shows: Barney. "One Barney" would equal one half hour, "Two Barneys" would be an hour, etc.

For years, even when the older children could tell time, they would still ask, "How many Barneys will it take to get there?" How do you tell time?

*~Laurie Dupar, PMHNP, RN, PCC Certified
ADHD Coach and Nurse Practitioner*

Laurie Dupar, PMHNP, RN, PCC, is a internationally-recognized expert on ADHD and the mother of four children, two with ADHD. You can reach her at www.coachingforADHD.com.

Couples & ADHD: Strategies to Strengthen Your Relationship

The need to be right can seem like a life or death feeling for adults with ADHD. Sometimes it may actually seem like a victory when we emotionally body-slam our partners to the ground, all in the name of proving that we were right. Injuring your partner leaves your lifetime co-pilot feeling upset and distant from you. Strategies to strengthen your partnership:

1. Show that you value your partner by listening first.

2. Put yourself in your partner's shoes and then act the way you would like to be treated.

3. Focus on the issues and *not* on being "right."

4. Avoid "always" and "never" statements and use "sometimes," "frequently," or "it seems like" instead.

5. Practice forgiveness and compassion, and remember to give positive feedback. Ask yourself this simple question: "Do I want to be *right*, or do I want to be *happy?*"

~ Sarah A. Ferman, L.M.F.T., P.C.C.
& Robert L. Wilford, Ph.D.

Sarah Ferman, L.M.F.T., P.C.C., & Robert Wilford, Ph.D., are leading ADHD Couples Consultants, helping ADHD Couples reconnect and create loving and enduring relationships. www.ADHDCouplesConsultants.com

SMART You - Achieving More with Goals

SMART goal help you achieve more. Use the tips below to make your goals SMART.

Specific: Be as specific as possible when writing goals to reduce your working memory load.

Measurable: When you measure each goal, you actually know when you achieve it. This is important to maintain direction and self-confidence.

Action-oriented: Having a goal that is action-oriented helps you determine the best action steps to achieve your goal.

Realistic: Making your goals realistic helps set you up for success. Unrealistic goals are frustrating and discouraging.

Time-bound: Set deadlines to maintain attention on your goals. If a goal is far into the future, set milestone dates to keep you on track.

As you work towards your goals, schedule goal tune-ups to review and revise goals periodically.

~Laura Rolands, ADHD Coach

Laura Rolands is an ADHD Coach who helps clients manage time, focus on priorities, pay attention, increase productivity and achieve goals. Learn more at www.MyAttentionCoach.com.

"Ready, Set ... Let Go!"

Helping your children become independent isn't just about coaching them to be self-sufficient. It's about learning to let go. And it's NOT easy! As parents, we know we should gradually "back off," but there are three things that get in our way:

1. We want to rescue our kid and make life a little easier.
2. We want to look "good" as parents. If our kids get average or poor grades, we take it personally.
3. We want it done...now. It's easier to do things ourselves.

These reactions are typical, normal, and not always helpful. Letting go is hard, but seeing your child take on increasing responsibility is quite the reward! To practice letting go:

• Pay attention to when you rescue.
• Choose one area to step back.
• Take baby steps.
• Talk with other parents.
• Create a contingency plan.

~ *Elaine Taylor-Klaus, CPCC, ACC, and Diane Dempster, MHSA, CPC, ACC*

ImpactADHD helps parents help kids. Elaine Taylor-Klaus & Diane Dempster provide reality-based training, with coaching to make it stick. We help your family thrive! http://www.ImpactADHD.com

Are You Ready to Change?

At the age of nine, I believed that my life could be a bestseller, if I wrote it. Now, at the age of 35, I was told to share my personal success story in 150 words! Short version of the long story: although I was diagnosed when I was 26, I decided to redesign my life when I started to college. I was feeling the urge to change, and I was ready! So, my success secrets are:

- Be aware of yourself.
- Be an initiative dreamer.
- Be a believer.
- Know your priorities.
- Have supportive friends.
- Ask for help.
- Be determined.
- Don't compare yourself with others.
- Don't forget every problem is an opportunity.
- Think before you act.
- Never give up!

~Pınar Kobaş, ADHD Expert

Pınar Kobaş, Mental Health Counselor and ADHD Expert with ADHD. She lives in Turkey.
www.dehbka.com ~ pkobas@dehbka.com

New Possibilities

Our son is nine years old and often struggles to understand the meaning and importance of our need for rules and control. My husband finds it a great challenge to be any other way. After a stare-down of 2 minutes, our son very calmly but firmly said, "I can do this all day; I will never get bored looking at what is behind your eyes." Later, I asked what he meant by that and why he would rather get into trouble than give in. He softly told me that he was often confused because the words and actions we parents and teachers use do not match our insides. He taught me that it is more important to live with integrity and pure intent than to live with fear. I now understand his fearlessness.

~Juliet Victor, Performance Coach

Juliet Victor, Certified Performance Coach specializing in transformation and behavioral coaching, and aspiring Consciousness Coach. Juliet.victor@vodamail.co.za

Couples & ADHD: "Just One More Thing"

Few things motivate the ADHD brain like trying to beat the clock and do "just one more thing." Time crunches cause the ADHD brain to release a rush of adrenaline that clarify your thinking and make you feel more capable. Motivated by adrenaline, it's easy to convince yourself that you can squeeze in one little stop on the way, one phone call before heading out, a quick look online while your partner finishes getting ready....yet somehow you're always late.

The solution is to first agree ahead of time to a policy of "no stopping on the way" or "no starting something while your partner finishes getting ready." Instead, let your partner know that you're ready and will be waiting by the door or that you will be driving directly to your destination. When the adrenaline rush passes, you will be ready and on time.

~ Sarah A. Ferman, L.M.F.T., P.C.C.
& Robert L. Wilford, Ph.D.

Sarah Ferman, L.M.F.T., P.C.C., & Robert Wilford, Ph.D., are leading ADHD Couples Consultants, helping ADHD Couples reconnect and create loving and enduring relationships. www.ADHDCouplesConsultants.com

Hidden Highlights

As an ADHD coach, some of my favorite clients are college students. Students are some of the most hard-working and persistent clients I have. Reading, typically lots of reading, is a big part of college. The volume of reading can be overwhelming, not to mention uninteresting. And uninteresting material is a big potential pitfall for many students. One clever student created the following strategy to keep herself focused and interested when doing assigned reading. When she first read through a text, she would highlight everything in yellow. Doing this helped her keep track of what she had read. Next, she would go back and highlight key pieces in blue, which turned green when put over the yellow, or with pink, which would also change colors over the original yellow. This use of highlighters and creative combinations of colors was fun, engaging and helped her keep on track with an otherwise painstaking job.

~Laurie Dupar, PMHNP, RN, PCC Certified
ADHD Coach and Nurse Practitioner

Laurie Dupar, PMHNP, RN, PCC, is an internationally-recognized ADHD expert, author and speaker. Find out more at www.coachingforadhd.com or (916) 791-1799.

Never Be Late Again!

You don't have to be the last person arriving at an event, "fashionably late!" Try these tips to improve your performance:

- Increase your estimate of travel, parking, and walking time needed by 50%.

- Set your alarm (computer, watch, telephone, kitchen timer) to warn you at least five minutes before you have to walk out the door.

- Bring something to read or study in case you arrive too early to walk in.

- If you still arrive late, revise your planned travel time by another 50%.

- Do this every time you have to be somewhere at a specific time!

- You will amaze your friends and co-workers!

~ Hervé J. LeBoeuf, III, Ph.D.

Dr. LeBoeuf, Life and ADHD Coach, believes people of all ages with ADHD can be successful by learning to work with their unique brains. HLeBoeuf@Gmail.com

Ask *Who* NOT *How*

Each of us, whether we have ADHD or not, are good at doing some things and not so good at doing others. The difference for people with ADHD is that they are less sure that it is completely normal to not be able to do everything well.

What often stops a person with ADHD from getting things done is that they get stuck in not knowing "how" to do something and spend hours, days or even years trying to figure it out.

Instead, ask "who" either knows how to do this or can do this better or easier than me. Pay a neighbor to mow your lawn weekly. Take all of your laundry to the dry cleaners. Use online grocery lists and simply "pick up" your shopping.

Spend your time and energy doing what you are brilliant at and let other people do what is their genius.

~Laurie Dupar, PMHNP, RN, PCC Certified ADHD Coach and Nurse Practitioner

Laurie Dupar, PMHNP, RN, PCC, is an internationally-recognized ADHD expert, author and speaker. www.coachingforadhd.com ~ (916) 791-1799

Know Your Boss's Priorities

Succeeding at work with ADHD can be a real challenge. In addition to improving your skill sets, knowing how to navigate the work environment is also crucial. Here's a tip: one of the keys to advancing your career is to get to know and align with your boss's top priorities. That advice may sound counter-intuitive if you already have plenty on your plate. Why worry about the boss's problems? And if your boss is a real jerk, why make him or her look good?

The problem is that the performance of your job is not the only thing your co-workers will judge. How you contribute to your department and/or the company is also important. So it doesn't serve you well to ignore what the boss wants to accomplish. If you help make your boss look good and help the company succeed, it raises your profile as well.

~Paul O'Connor, MCC

Paul O'Connor coaches business executives with ADHD. He is a Master Certified Coach, secretary of the Professional Association of ADHD Coaches, based in Atlanta. (404) 377-4712. paul@EnergyForLifeCoach.com ~ www.EnergyForLifeCoach.com

Quarantine Useless Negativity with the 5-Minute Rule of Rumination

Are you a ruminator, constantly fretting about the past or future in a way that doesn't constructively accomplish anything? Ruminating about what you SHOULD have done or said, or how you MIGHT fail in the future, accomplishes nothing and sucks up time better spent in productivity or relaxation. The problem is, rumination is a brain habit that feeds on itself. The more you hyper-focus on anxious thoughts, the more easily your brain slides into negative self-talk, making it ever more difficult to get into real problem-solving.

Apply the **5-Minute Rule of Rumination**: Assign your unproductive obsession the same 5-minute period each day.

ONLY allow yourself to think about it in those five minutes, and don't set reminders. Chances are, most days you'll forget to obsess during the assigned time!

~Bonnie Mincu, MA, MBA, ADHD Coach

Bonnie Mincu, Senior Certified ADHD Coach, helps you maximize your productivity and income potential. In-depth programs on specific ADD challenges to reach your goals are available at www.thrivewithadd.com.

A Little Life Lesson on Learning and Living

Learn all you can. Learn about ADHD and how it affects you. The more you know about how your brain works, the more you can harness its power to be successful. Everyone has an Achilles heel. Maybe yours is disorganization, impulsive spending, poor time management, or stress. Learn to recognize it before it takes you down. Always keep watch and guard against it so you don't get blindsided. Get help when you need to. If you could solve the problem yourself, it wouldn't be called a problem. Always keep learning. A philosopher once said you never step in the same river twice. Things change, people change, life happens. Life will keep throwing new challenges at you. You will make mistakes, but keep learning and growing each time. Remember, it's your life. Don't just pass the time like a study hall. Live each day to bring you closer to the life you want.

~Rose Smith, M. Ed.

Rose Smith, M. Ed. For more helpful hints and random reflections, please visit http://RandomReflectionsbyRose.wordpress.com/.

There's Always Tomorrow

Raising four children, including two with ADHD, there were many days when I felt like I had completely failed. There were days when I'd said or done the wrong thing, gotten angry, and completely missed an opportunity to be the parent I wanted to be. As an ADHD coach, working with parents and families, I often hear the same disappointment from my clients. More than anything, parents want to support and help their children. There are just some days that it doesn't work out that way.

Something I learned is that with parenting, there is always tomorrow. Tomorrow, whether we're ready or not, we will get another chance with our ADHD children, to practice being patient, understanding and keeping our cool.

Just as we hope our ADHD children will be given another chance for "good" days, we will be waking up right beside them with the same opportunity to try again.

~Laurie Dupar, PMHNP, RN, PCC Certified
ADHD Coach and Nurse Practitioner

Laurie Dupar, a psychiatric nurse practitioner and professionally certified coach for nine years, lives in the greater Sacramento, CA area. (916) 791-1799

"Be yourself, that is something you can do better than anyone else. Listen to that inner voice and bravely follow it."

~ Anonymous

Seven Survival Skills to Succeed with ADD in Business

In business? Here are seven things you must know:

1. Know your organization's culture and policies to avoid stepping on landmines as you unleash your creativity.

2. Cherish the value of the...PAUSE; rather than blurting opinions on controversial issues, run your ideas by a trusted colleague first.

3. Examine your assumptions to deepen understanding.

4. Practice saying "no" diplomatically, e.g., "Let me think about it," rather than taking on too much.

5. Follow through on projects. Delegate when possible. Use tracking tools: calendars, timers, software.

6. Build collaborative relationships. Find ways to appreciate, not just tolerate, others' differences.

7. Discover how to *really* listen, which supports all of the above. Stay open to surprise!

~ *"Mid-Life Alchemist"*

"Mid-Life Alchemist" specializes in helping professional women create "retirement jobs" that offer more freedom and prosperity while unleashing their inner brilliance. Anne@ClarityAtTheCrossroads.com ~ (978)-371-8077

Creating Conflict to Avoid Conflict: How Us ADHD Individuals Deal with Sticky Situations

As an adult with ADHD as well as a professional that helps individuals with ADHD, one of my favorite strategies to get out of tricky situations is to create conflict to avoid conflict, or make the situation about everything else. For example, when a child doesn't do his or her homework, it often becomes about things like the parent distracting the child as opposed to the actual homework. Without even realizing it, parents will get sucked into this little battle. It then becomes about everything else except the homework. In order to avoid this type of argument, it is important to keep it about homework. When a child makes it about everything else, stay on message. While this isn't always easy to execute, one suggestion is to write down the issue and bring the conversation back to that topic. Keep saying, "What does this have to do with your homework?"

~Jonathan D. Carroll, M.A.

Jonathan D. Carroll is considered an expert on ADHD and works as a coach in the Chicagoland area. Please visit http://www.adhdcoachchicago.com for more information

Tips on Paying Attention During a Lecture or Presentation

When you attend a lecture, presentation or workshop, do you worry about paying attention? Or your behavior? Here are some tips to help you:

- Sit in the front row. This will help you make a better connection with the speaker, as well as force you to be more attentive.

- Take notes. Taking notes will help you pay attention and keep you on track with what is going on.

- Think of questions. Listen with the idea of asking a question in mind. This will also help you stay in tune with the speaker. Wait until the speaker asks for questions before you speak, and ask yourself if your question is really appropriate, or if you are just looking for a chance to speak. Do not use your time to tell a personal story or an anecdote. Be creative and try to think of more ways to stay in the game.

~Abigail Wurf, M.Ed., CLC

Abigail Wurf coaches executives, entrepreneurs, couples and other adults affected by ADHD, as well as high school and college students. Serving Washington DC and nationally. awurf@verizon.net ~ abigailwurf.com ~ 202-244-2234

Muscle + Music + Beer = Clean House

A highly successful, handsome bachelor I know uses his ADHD traits to live large and in charge. He tackles his business and his life with gusto and the finesse of James Bond, except when it comes to the mundane task of cleaning house. When his living space reaches 100 on the bachelor pad slob scale, he activates his mind and his muscles by combining his workout with elbow grease. The dumb bells come out, the music is turned up and a cold beer is opened. He knocks out two minutes of dreaded housework between 8 sets each of bicep curls, push-ups and/or military press. Moving at the speed of lightning gives him the sense of urgency needed to keep this unique form of circuit training a top priority. The result is a fit physique and, after 32-48 minutes of manic home maintenance, his house is now Bond-girl ready.

~Nancy Bean, Certified ADHD Coach, Professional Organizer, Interior Designer

Nancy Bean builds relationships between people, places and spaces, helping clients create change in their lives. SIMPLIFY by DESIGN: Certified ADHD Coach, Designer/Organizer. simplify@nancybean.com

"Eye of the Tiger" Motivation

One of the problems with "getting motivated" is that we haven't bothered to put ourselves into a positive mental state. We're so focused on how hard it's going to be, we talk ourselves out of it. Have you ever watched an individual in a sports competition talk to themselves? They're having full-on conversations completely by themselves, and it all involves giving themselves a pep talk. So try this: Instead of worrying how hard it's going to be, start talking to yourself about how much fun it's going to be, how you've got what it takes, all sorts of positive motivating talk. Pace back and forth. Put on some exciting music like "Eye of the Tiger." Have your own "huddle up pep talk." And then dive in. I promise you it will be easier to start; and once you've started, the ball will keep rolling.

~Roger DeWitt, PCC, BCC

Roger DeWitt, PCC, BCC, ADHD Coach for Creative Executives and the Entertainment Industry. www.adhdcoachnyc.com

Did I or Didn't I...?

Remember to take my ADHD medication today? For many, ADHD medication can make the difference between a great day and a day of chaos, forgetting, spinning and overwhelm. If ADHD medications are part of your management strategies, taking your ADHD medications consistently is key.

Place it by your bedside with a glass of water and take right when you get up in the morning

• "Attach" the routine of taking the medication with another existing habit, such as brushing your teeth, drinking your morning cup of coffee or eating breakfast

• Set alarm reminders on your phone for afternoon doses

• Organize your medications in a daily pill box so if you can't remember if you took them today, one peek will let you know "yay" or "nay"

• Stash an extra dose for those "forgot" days in your purse, backpack or wallet

~ Laurie Dupar, Mental Health Nurse Practitioner

Laurie Dupar is a trained Psychiatric Mental Health Nurse Practitioner and Senior Certified ADHD Coach. Reach her at www.coachingforadhd.com or (916) 791-1799.

A Clean and Clear Space: Within and Without

When I was in first grade, my teacher expressed her regret because there wasn't a test for distractibility; that was a test she was sure I would ace. At the age of thirty, I did ace it. Well, not really, but I was diagnosed with ADHD, which explained a lot. Back when I was in first grade, they didn't know about ADHD.

Years later, I limit distractibility. How? I create what I think of as clean and clear space, within and without. I need to eliminate distracters, like sound, clutter, and thoughts, both in my environment and in my mind, that make it hard to focus. Of course, some people need a steady sound to block out distractions; they use white sound machines or calming music. Just ask yourself how you can create a clean and clear space in your mind and environment, and you'll be all set.

~Abigail Wurf, M.Ed., CLC

Abigail Wurf coaches executives, entrepreneurs, couples and other adults affected by ADHD, as well as high school and college students. Serving Washington DC and nationally. awurf@verizon.net ~ abigailwurf.com ~ (202) 244-2234

Your ADD Traits Do Not Control You

You control you. Your ADD traits may give you a propensity to behave in certain ways, but they can't force you to do anything. If a behavior isn't getting you the result you want, you can override it.

For example, you may blurt things out in meetings because you are afraid you will lose a thought; however, that may not serve you well in the long run if it turns others off. So, next time, you may make a choice to write down your thoughts on a notepad and only voice them at an appropriate moment. You just changed your behavior. You didn't let a tendency to behave a certain way control your life. Remember: you are not your ADD, you are you. You're this wonderful person with tremendous gifts and strengths who can do great things in this world. You choose how you respond.

~Paul O'Connor, MCC

Paul O'Connor coaches business executives with ADHD. He is a Master Certified Coach, secretary of the Professional Association of ADHD Coaches, based in Atlanta. (404) 377-4712 paul@EnergyForLifeCoach.com ~ www.EnergyForLifeCoach.com

DON'T Make a Decision! Leave it to Chance

I tend to get lost in the process of weighing options. My mother said it was because I'm a Libra, but I think it's because of the ADHD. The pressure of having to make the right decision shuts me down faster than anything. How much is enough information? Have I really exhausted all of my options? The truth is, those questions are irrelevant and meaningless because whatever result I get, I can respond to and adapt. That I know. So, to make a decision, I play a game: 1) I give myself the time limit; 2) I narrow my choices to a few...no more than 4; and 3) I have someone or something else make the decision. Draw one out of a hat. Use a random number generator. Tell someone else to pick. Flip a coin. And that's my decision. It's usually the right one...whatever that means. Try it!

~Roger DeWitt, PCC, BCC

Roger DeWitt, PCC, BCC, ADHD Coach for Creative Executives and the Entertainment Industry. www.adhdcoachnyc.com

Creatively Organized: Papers and Email

How to organize your paperwork:

- De-clutter email quickly: Rearrange your in-box by putting the "from" list into alphabetical order. Delete batches of spam email and unsubscribe from each as you move through the list.

- Google "paper retention guidelines" to help you decide which papers to keep and for how long.

- Sort paper into 4 piles: Shred, Recycle, Keep to file, Deal with it now. Sit next to a shredder and recycle container when you go through bags or papers (or miles of files), one bag or folder at a time.

- Remember, for every hour you spend de-cluttering, you need an hour to put away what you keep.

~Dr. Regina Lark, Ph.D., CPO

Dr. Regina Lark, Certified Professional Organizer, specializes in de-cluttering and organizing for the ADD/ADHD brain. www.AClearPath.net ~ regina@AClearPath.net

Helpful Habits: By the Door & on the Floor the Night Before

How often have you rushed out in the morning and left something behind: a book, folder, bag, or file that you had intended to take along?

Forgetting about and leaving things behind is certainly one of the ways that ADHD shows up in my life. Here is one of my *HELPFUL HABITS* that I developed years ago, long before I learned that I had AD/HD. This strategy still works for me: I simply place all the items that I plan to take with me the next morning directly *by the door & on the floor the night before.*

Chances are that I will remember the items if I have to **first trip over** them before I can actually get out the door. Of course, nothing is foolproof; I still forget things when I forget to follow my own advice.

~Monika Pompetzki, ADHD Coach

Monika Pompetzki, BSc, MEd, AD/HD, academic, & life coach focused on creating HELPFUL HABITS that can make life a little easier. www.add-adhdCoaching.com ~ monika@add-adhdCoaching.com ~ (905) 336-8330

Do You Suffer from Time Zone Dyscalculia?

In today's world, scheduling calls, meetings or appointments in different time zones is common. Keeping track of them accurately can be a nightmare! In fact, I am sure I have what I fondly call "time zone dyscalculia!" I always ended up miscalculating the hours and inevitably called at the wrong time. In order to keep mine and my client's sanity, I came up with the strategies below:

- Check out smart phone apps for "time zone calculators"
- Keep a "time zone map" handy
- Use an appointment-scheduling system (www.timedriver.com is my favorite)
- Set some old-fashioned wall clocks to the most common time zones you work with

Never suffer from Time Zone Dyscalculia again!

~Laurie Dupar, ADHD Coach, Speaker & Author

Laurie Dupar is an internationally-recognized ADHD Coach, speaker and author. You can reach her at www.coachingforadhd.com or (916) 791-1799.

Of Fruit and Filing

Fruit and filing: two related, but seemingly unrelated, challenges that plague people with ADHD every day. The root of both challenges is their containers: the crisper and the filing cabinet. Closed containers create a powerful barrier to someone with ADHD. Sometimes having to open something can turn us off to an idea, even before it fully forms in our head, particularly if it's as boring as filing. Also, containers block our view of the items within, which can keep us from remembering the contents. Visual cues help us remember! How can we overcome this phenomenon? Keep things in plain sight. Put apples on the shelf instead of in the crisper. Use milk crates to file documents. They'll be easy to access and easy to see. Use the visual cue of multicolored folders to differentiate one file from another. Keeping things in plain sight = a healthier, more organized you.

~Brendan Mahan, M.Ed.

Brendan Mahan, M.Ed. is an ADHD coach specializing in helping students with ADHD and their families find success in school and at home. mahancoaching@gmail.com.

Calming the Racy Brain Game

To calm a racy mind, write down all of your ideas on paper as they come up. Try to completely drain your brain. You can even make this a game by using a timer and noting your time beside each "race." Try to beat your past record for the most ideas in the same amount of time. For me, once the ideas are out of my head, I can relax. Once in a while, you can re-read some of your races from the past week. You might find patterns, great ideas you want to explore, common worries/fears that keep coming up, and more.

~Diane Frescura

When I Need to Remember...

When I need to remember to do something, I say it out loud. For example: "I need to remember the class at 10:00 this morning."

Or when I put my glasses down, I might say, "I am putting my glasses on the end table." Also, when trying to remember a phone number or any numbers, I visualize a dialer on a phone. Then place the numbers in their spots.

Here is a fun one. When I want to remember to take something with me from the refrigerator/freezer, I put the keys in the refrigerator/freezer to help me remember. I have even taken food over to a friend's house and put it all in their refrigerator/freezer so I do not forget to take it when I go home.

Always the LAUNCH PAD by the door.

~Karen Rosie

Pinterest on Purpose

Since the ADHD brain likes to seek stimulation, we often spend time on-line looking, searching and playing. It's fun. But it's neither urgent nor important, so it can get in the way of our daily tasks and overall life progress. One site on which you can find visual stimulation, learn, grow and have fun at the same time is Pinterest.

It's like a visual bulletin board of valuable information from infographics to eating well, from how to change your oil to what to wear this season. When you Pinterest on purpose, you categorize your finds in clusters to which you can return when you need to know or do something. Pinterest is the perfect visual catalogue for ADHD, and you can do it without guilt. So, click, like and categorize to your heart's content. Just make sure you circle back and use what you have learned.

~Lynne Kenney, Psy.D.

Lynne Kenney, Psy.D., is a mother of two, a practicing pediatric psychologist in Scottsdale, AZ, and the creator of The Family Coach Method. Her NEW co-authored book, *Time-In not Time-Out*, is available this Fall on Kindle. For more visit www.lynnekenney.com.

More "Being" and Less "Doing"

Having lived in six different countries, I can say that our culture is primarily a "to do "culture versus a "to be" one. I believe that both of those are important and necessary but what is missing out here is the balance between the two. In the case of a family with one or more members diagnosed with ADHD, the balance between the "to do" and "to be" is extremely important. Family members should have some down time both together and independently in order to best take care of themselves, their family and to be able to enjoy each other. Although being active is extremely important for individuals with ADHD, so too is the quiet time. I suggest that you give it a try for few weeks and see how the family dynamic changes for the better.

~Roya Kravetz, ADHD Coach and Consultant

Roya Kravetz is a Credentialed Life Coach who specializes in ADHD Coaching and Consulting. Roya strongly believes in a strength-based coaching approach. She coaches in 3 languages and is internationally recognized. www.adhdsuccesscoaching.com

Road Rage to Road Engaged!

With statistics showing that drivers with ADHD are four times more likely than others to be involved in car accidents and be ticketed for driving violations, finding ways to keep focused yet relaxed behind the wheel is important!

Interestingly, I have had drivers describe everything from being too focused and frustrated by what is happening outside their car to losing focus in the car because of boredom. Some of my clients' favorite strategies to help them stay engaged in safe driving include:

- Listen to soothing white noise or nature sounds
- Listen to informational CD's from ADHD telesummits/classes/workshops
- Always plan for unexpected delays
- Change the music/tape you listen to in your car if you find your mind drifting
- Map out a new course to your destination if you find that the monotony of the same route has you zoning out at the wheel

~Laurie Dupar, ADHD Coach, Speaker & Author

Laurie Dupar, internationally-recognized ADHD expert, speaker and author. She lives near Sacramento, California. You can reach her at Laurie@coachingforadhd.com or (916) 791-1799.

When You Don't Want to Lose Something...

If you absolutely, positively *cannot* afford lose something (e.g., license renewal paper that is due in two months, unsigned divorce decree, notice of an important event), post it on the front of the refrigerator. Tape it down if you have to. You'll see it every day and, seriously, when's the last time you lost the refrigerator?

~Linda

Big Rewards from Small Successes

Long-term goals are hard to reach. How do you keep yourself going every day, when the goal is so far off? Choose a smaller goal that, when accomplished daily, will get you the result you want, even far in the future. Maintain your everyday motivation by giving yourself a smaller daily reward, leading to an even bigger reward when you are done.

For example, consider weight loss. Full-on diets are tough to keep. Instead, eliminate one thing, like snacking. It's a goal that is easier to maintain every day, but with the same long-term result. Then, pay yourself a small amount every day that you don't snack, maybe a dollar or two. Put it in a jar to save. When you've reached your goal weight, use your money to treat yourself to a luxury item.

No snacks = weight loss. Daily reward = big payoff. And long-term goal success.

~ Jeffrey S. Katz, Ph.D., Clinical Psychologist

Dr. Jeffrey Katz, clinical psychologist, expert in the evaluation and treatment of AD/HD, learning and behavior problems. Helping individuals and families to succeed. www.DrJeffreyKatz.com

The Key to Task Completion

When my sons and I are overwhelmed with a task, such as cleaning up, I have discovered one way that helps us tackle it: disregarding the big picture, pick up the first thing we see or run into, or the thing closest or on top, and decide to put it in some logical place. We then move on to the next thing, without regard to any real organizing techniques, or sorting, or compiling, or anything else that might make sense or be most practical to most people. That way, we eventually whittle down piles of mess without being so stuck because we don't know where to start.

~Anonymous

The Importance of Stimulation

A child with ADHD has a brain that seeks stimulation. This happens because their brain has a chemical deficiency, and stimulation causes the brain to manufacture chemicals it needs. Stimulation can be physical or cognitive, and it can be positive or negative. It can come in the form of playing a sport, jumping on a trampoline, arguing with a parent or sibling, playing an educational computer game, having a temper tantrum, or being engaged in something that is of high interest. Ensure that your child is getting enough positive physical and cognitive stimulation every day to help balance their brain chemicals.

~Judith Champion, MSW, ACG

Judith Champion, MSW, ACG, ADHD Family Coach and Educator. ADHD affects the whole family. Coaching for parents, children and adults. www.ADHDAssociates.com ~ judith@judithchampion.com

ADHD is an Explanation, Not an Excuse

I completely understand how difficult it is to have a child with ADHD. In fact, I have two. As a parent, I wanted my children to know that they, not their ADHD, were responsible for their behavior. And also that their ADHD was not an excuse for being able to do or not do something. Living with ADHD explains why some things are more difficult, but it is never a reason why someone can or can't do something.

We are more than just our ADHD. Everyone, ADHD or not, has their innate personal strengths and challenges. Having ADHD explains why it may take longer to learn something, be harder to sit still, become more easily overwhelmed, and say or do things impulsively, but it is never an excuse.

~Laurie Dupar, PMHNP, RN, PCC, Certified ADHD Coach and Nurse Practitioner

Laurie Dupar is a Certified ADHD Coach, trained psychiatric nurse practitioner, author and speaker. You can contact her at www.coachingforadhd.com or (916) 791 1799.

Couples & ADHD: Does Your Brain Skip the Word No?

Susan and her partner were driving to meet their best friends for a surprise birthday celebration at a new five-star restaurant. It was critical they arrive on time. To help, Susan's partner navigated by giving her directions. As they come to a fork in the freeway, Susan asked, "Which one do I take?" Her partner blurted, "Don't take 585," and Susan proceeds to merge right onto highway 585, as her partner started yelling "Not 585, not 585!"

When he asked her, "Why didn't you take the 22?" she responded, "You said take the 585!" Adults with ADHD tend to overlook negative interjections like "no" and "don't," because we over-focus on listening to the key words in a request. It is better to focus on what you *want* your partner to do or remember when communicating a request (*not* on what you *don't* want them to do).

~ Sarah A. Ferman, L.M.F.T., P.C.C.
& Robert L. Wilford, Ph.D.

Sarah Ferman, L.M.F.T., P.C.C., & Robert Wilford, Ph.D., are leading ADHD Couples Consultants, helping ADHD couples reconnect and create loving and enduring relationships. www.ADHDCouplesConsultants.com

All Facts Aren't

Hundreds of years ago, it was an obvious fact to mankind that Earth was the center of the universe. It was reclassified to be a belief when we realized Earth orbits the sun and, thus, the sun was the center of our universe. This, too, was reclassified from fact to fiction when we realized our solar system rotates around the center of the galaxy. Now, we realize our galaxy is just one of many, and the notion that the center of the galaxy is the center of the universe has been reclassified. Question is: Are facts really facts? Something to think about!

~Jeff Copper, MBA, PCC, ACG, CPCC

Jeff Copper, MBA, PCC, ACG, CPCC, is an attention coach, founder of DIG Coaching Practice, and host of Attention Talk Radio...Your ADHD Information Station! www.digcoaching.com

Create a New Habit

Creating a new habit takes time and consistency; however, if you can focus on the following seven steps, you will be well on your way to creating permanent change in your life.

1. **Commit to only thirty days.**

2. **Do it daily.**

3. **Start small and simple:** Don't try to completely change your life in one day.

4. **Connect it:** Associate a new behavior with something you already do every day.

5. **Be imperfect:** Change can take multiple tries.

6. **Know the pleasure and the pain:** Know the benefits of making a change and the consequences of not changing.

7. **Begin again:** At about two weeks into a new habit, it can be easy to forget. Place reminders around and if you happen to miss a few days, you always get another chance by going back to step number one!

~*Laurie Dupar, PMHNP, RN, PCC, Certified ADHD Coach*

Laurie Dupar is a Certified ADHD Coach and internationally- known ADHD expert. Connect with her at (916) 791-1799 or www.coachingforadhd.com.

Stop Procrastinating and Dare to Be (Gulp!) Average

ADHD folks procrastinate for some very good reasons. They can't find their pens. They forgot to check the time and they want the final result to be *perfect*. Why? Because we have screwed up so many times that we think our latest effort must exceed not only our previous attempts, but everyone else's attempts, too. When we demand perfection of ourselves, we are paralyzed. We know intellectually that being perfect is a myth, yet we still expect it of ourselves. Next time you're paralyzed by perfection, dare to be (gulp) average. Yep, average. Let yourself do only an "adequate" job instead of a stellar job. Only you will know the difference and the truth is that getting DONE by doing an average job is 100% better than missing the deadline because you're aiming for perfection. Just ask your boss. I dare you!

~Linda Roggli, PCC

Linda Roggli, PCC; award-winning author of *Confessions of an ADDiva - Midlife in the Non-Linear Lane* and ADHD coach/retreat facilitator, supporting women 40-and-better at www.addiva.net.

Velcro or Teflon?

Sometimes our minds can get stuck on an idea or feeling and we just can't seem to let it go. It's as though we have a Velcro mind and can't pull it apart to let go. When we ruminate, we're in Velcro mind, but when we're in hyperfocus, we may also be in Velcro mind. Velcro mind can be useful or harmful, depending on the situation. The same is true of Teflon mind. Sometimes, when we're trying to learn or remember something, it feels like our mind is made of Teflon and nothing sticks. When our children are screaming at us, having a Teflon mind can be a very good thing; their hurtful words just don't stick. So, we have both a Velcro mind and a Teflon mind, and it's up to us to notice the situation and choose which would be most useful to us in the moment. When that ruminative thought appears, shift to Teflon mind and let it slide away!

~Barbara Luther, Master Certified Coach

Barbara Luther, President, Professional Association of ADHD Coaches, www.PAACCoaches.org. Director of Training, ADD Coach Academy, www.addca.com. Master Certified ADHD Coach.
www.WindBeneathYourWings.com ~ www.SoaringCoachesCircle.com
St. Louis, MO ~ 573-340-3559

Structure Your Time To Get More Done

Do you structure your time? Or are you free to pretty much do anything at any time, and if so, how's that working for you? If it's not working so well, you're not alone. Living without some kind of structure can be a real handicap for people with ADHD. The solution is to be disciplined about structuring your time so that you're not all over the place. For instance:

- Treat academics like a 9-5 job. Save other activities for evenings and weekends.

- Mark on your agenda the hours you are typically most creative. Only do work requiring creativity in that block of time. Everything else can wait its turn.

- Spend your best hours planning, strategizing, and doing work that is PROactive. Don't waste your best hours on email. Save easier REactive tasks for when your attention is beginning to fade.

~Sarah D. Wright, M.S., A.C.T.

Nationally-known ADHD coach Sarah D. Wright specializes in helping professionals in small businesses get on track and get going. FocusForEffectiveness.com ~ Sarah@FocusForEffectiveness.com (858) 408-9338.

Are You "Time Blind"?

"Where did the time go?" Lack of time awareness, not having a sense of time passing, or not being able to accurately estimate how long something will take to do are common challenges for people ADHD. Most don't realize that their procrastination, overwhelm or inability to get things done is related to this "time blindness."

Being "time blind" is very real and can be understood by comparing it to people who are color blind. People who are color blind may never be able to differentiate between colors, but they learn strategies to compensate.

Being time blind is the same. Make sure your environment is full of time reminders. Go back to wearing a watch. Use alarms on your phone to go off every hour. Place analog clocks (the ones with hands) everywhere, including the bathroom, shower, garage and even your car.

~Laurie Dupar, PMHNP, RN, PCC, Certified ADHD Coach and Nurse Practitioner

Laurie Dupar is an internationally-recognized ADHD expert, speaker and author of *Unlock the Secrets to Your Entrepreneurial Brian Style.* www.coachingforadhd.com ~ (916) 791-1799

HIGHLY DISTRACTIBLE?
An Interruption Log Can
Help You Cope

I keep steno pads in the kitchen, on my desk, and by my computer, all of which are areas where I'm often pulled off task by distractions or interruptions. The spiral binding holds my pencil. *Before* I shift focus, I take a few seconds to jot down enough about where I was to hit the ground running on my return. Why take up cognitive bandwidth on "remembering" when we can simply check the log? The action of writing it down adds modalities, increasing the likelihood we'll remember to return. *Be sure* to cross out the last entry on return to your task. That helps strengthen the "I need to get back to what I was doing" pathways in your brain. I find this system especially effective with those "quick" interruptions I used to believe I could handle without a system. A trip to the bathroom no longer derails my day! See ADDandSoMuchMore.com for more about distractibility.

~Madelyn Griffith-Haynie, CTP, CMC, A.C.T., MCC, SCAC

Madelyn Griffith-Haynie, multi-certified LifeCoaching pioneer, founded The Optimal Functioning Institute™, the earth's first ADD-specific coach training program. Graduates have spread her strategies world-wide. mgh@addcoach.com

The Study Cube

Studying can be difficult and BORING for students with ADHD. My favorite study strategy, The Study Cube, comes from a 7th grade student to whom I dedicate this article. Actually, The Study Cube is a compilation of six strategies that work well for an individual student. Complete the following steps to create The Study Cube for yourself or your favorite student:

1. Identify six strategies that work well for you or ones you want to try.
2. Find a box with approximately the same size sides for your cube.
3. Cover the cube with colorful paper.
4. Put one strategy on each side of the cube. Be creative. Use your favorite computer program or web images to help add details.
5. When it is time to study, roll The Study Cube and use the strategy ends up on top when it stops rolling.

~Laura Rolands, ADHD Coach

Laura Rolands is an ADHD Coach who regularly helps student clients decide which study skills work best for them. Contact Laura at www.MyAttentionCoach.com.

Budget Your Kindle Clicks

I love my Amazon Kindle. It fits in my purse and I always have my favorite books to read. When I get the urge to read the "hottest" book or play a game, it is so easy to find something new in one click. This is a dream...but like all dreams, nightmares can occur, showing up as BILLS at the end of the month. Although, to my recollection, many of the books I download are FREE, there are many that are *only* $.99, therefore I click away! To control my purchases, I bought Amazon Kindle Gift Cards and downloaded them onto my Kindle. Now, whenever I make a purchase, I am in control of what I am spending and I'm more conscious of my impulse purchases. My "nightmare" has returned to being my "dream" once again. Morale of the story: Gift cards help control budget and spending!

~Cindy Giardina, PCC

Cindy Giardina is a Professional Certified Coach, specializing in adults and students with ADHD. cindy@kaleidoscope-coaching.com ~ (973) 694-5077

Don't SHOULD on Yourself

Eliminate the word "should" from your vocabulary. "Should" implies a law that you have enforced upon yourself; even worse, it's a law only you are aware of.

For example, there is no law stating you have to go to the gym. So if you say "I *should* go to the gym," and as a result you do go to the gym, you cannot reward yourself because you made it law. Come Friday, if you haven't gone to the gym, you are down on yourself because you have broken one of your laws to live by.

What to do?

Bring power back to your decision making. When you notice that you are *should*ing on yourself, STOP and rephrase your sentence to: "I want to go to the gym" or "I will go to the gym." You will notice you are no longer organizing your life around worry and you will experience lowered anxiety.

~Coach Madeleine Cote, ACG

Coach Maddy is an ADHD Coach specializing in ADHD students and their families. She helps you get control back in your life. www.thecenterofattentionforadd.com

Attitudes for ADHD Mastery

Mantras to keep a positive attitude:

I have unique talents and creative gifts to offer the world.

My brain functions quite well, just differently.

I am willing and able to ask for help.

I access outsources, resources and the source of inner wisdom. When things change, I can adjust and make a new plan easily. Exercise, sleep, nutrition and mindfulness keep my brain well nourished.

I extend kindness and understanding to those around me.

I know my strengths and use them to the best of my ability.

I strive to succeed in the face of challenge, even if it means step by step.

There is a difference between 'I am ADHD' and 'I have ADHD'; I choose the latter.

I acknowledge and appreciate those in my life.

I celebrate my life! Including both accomplishments to be proud of and mistakes that help me grow.

~Melissa Fahrney, M.A., CPC

Melissa Fahrney, certified ADHD Coach & School Psychologist, specializes in heart-centered coaching for youth and adults. "Add Heart Power and Power the Mind" ~ www.addheartworks.com

Awareness Creation

I have a very interesting family, and my life is never boring, I often pray for some peace and quiet in the chaos of our home. I have learned, when dealing with people, that one size does *not* fit all, and my family tests this to the limit. For years, I have been asking myself and others what the purpose could be for these interesting, challenging individuals to be here, as I believe nothing happens by accident and without reason. What has come to me this year is the reality that one cannot work with, live with, teach, love or know anyone with ADD or ADHD without becoming more aware, conscious and accountable for all that you say, do and stand for.

~Juliet Victor, Performance Coach

Juliet Victor, Certified Performance Coach specializing in transformation and behavioral coaching, and aspiring Consciousness Coach. Juliet.victor@vodamail.co.za

Don't Miss a Step: Celebrate!

A familiar strategy for reaching goals is to break them down into smaller chunks and complete those smaller steps until the goal is reached. First step: assess the situation. The second step is to set the goal. Third step: break the goal into smaller, doable steps. Fourth step is completion.

We make plans weekly. Daily, we check and re-check our to-do lists and breathe a sigh of relief when we can see that we are making progress. And after reaching step four, we return to step one and ask, "Okay, what's next?"

Hold on. Stop right there. Something's missing!

There is actually a very important fifth step. Step five is where we *celebrate* our achievements! Have fun, rejoice, pat ourselves on the back and even make merry! Do whatever it is that says "Yay, me!" And only then, after you've celebrated, should you go on to your next "to do."

~Laurie Dupar, PMHNP, RN, PCC, Certified
ADHD Coach and Nurse Practitioner

Laurie Dupar, PMHNP, RN, PCC, is an internationally-recognized ADHD expert, coach and speaker. Contact her at (916) 791-1799 or www.coachingforadhd.com.

"Success means having the courage, the determination and the will to become the person you were meant to be."

~ George Sheean

ADHD and the External Brain

Nothing creates stress in the ADHD brain like trying to remember things. In our daily lives, we're constantly making commitments with ourselves or others by agreeing to do things or agreeing to be somewhere at a certain place and time. Keeping track of these commitments in our head can create a tremendous amount of stress.

Enter the External Brain. The brain is a great place to have ideas but a terrible place to manage them. The purpose of an external brain is to have a trusted system where all of these commitments are captured. Simple is better! The ideal external brain consists of a single calendar for appointments and a single list-management tool for other commitments. The key in convincing our internal brain to let go is to make sure everything makes it onto our list and that we review it often enough to convince our brain to let go.

~Jay Carter, MBA, ACG

Jay Carter is an adult ADHD coach specializing in personal productivity and workplace issues. Learn more about Jay's practice at www.hyperfocusedcoaching.com or jaycarter@hyperfocusedcoaching.com.

Outlook, Folders and Tasks...Oh My! Email Management for the Organizationally Challenged

Much like Dorothy in The Wizard of Oz feared the forest, navigating and managing our inbox can be a scary and daunting endeavor. It is important to keep in mind the big picture, as well as the daily details. This simple *Reply-Sort-Revisit* system helps you to do both:

- **Reply** to EVERY email (even junk). Something as simple as "Got it" works. This adds a copy of every email to your sent folder.
- **Sort**: Once you reply, either: Delete (junk) or sort to a folder.
- **Revisit:** Create a WIP (Work In Progress) folder in your Inbox. Under the WIP folder create 5 subfolders labeled Monday-Friday. If an email action item is due in 2 weeks or less, add it to one of the weekday subfolders. Check these on the corresponding days to ensure that small things don't get lost in the inbox! Use inbox for HOT items only.

~Shaun Roney, CEO

Shaun Roney is the owner of Spicey Living Virtual Assistant Services. Details and pictures of the Reply-Sort-Revisit system can be found on the website www.varietythespiceoflife.com.

No Beginning, No End!

One of my clients noticed that when she made her processes circular, with no beginning and no end, she could jump in and start without difficulty. When processes were linear, with a beginning and end, she had a hard time getting started. An example might look like this: Read and Research, Gather Data, Run Reports, Create Graphics, Create Presentation, Make Client Call. You can start at any one of these points as long as you do them all at some time during the process. Such processes can be used for daily routines, projects or individual processes. How can you create your own circular process? See if it helps you get started on things you tend to procrastinate about.

~Deb Bollom, ADHD & Life Coach

Deb Bollom, Certified ADHD Coach, works with entrepreneurs and adults who hate details and feel overwhelmed to help them discover their strengths and create ways to move forward. www.D5Coaching.com

Stop Asking For Permission

If you don't have what you truly want, use these six steps to give yourself permission to have what you desire:

1. **Get a guide** – You'll give yourself permission, but most people need a guide who knows the terrain and can assist you to the gateway.

2. **Explore** and **Envision** – Pick an area in your life and explore what you really want. What would life be like if you had what you wanted in this area?

3. **Identify** your programming (reasons, rationalizations and excuses) that say you can't have what you want.

4. **Give** yourself a resource who will say, "Go for it!" Let them, real or imagined, give you permission until you're ready to give it to yourself.

5. **Commit.** Write: "**I give myself permission to...**" (fill in). Sign and date it.

6. **Act** – Identify what you want and then take the next step towards having it.

~ *Michael Tertes, CEO*

Michael Tertes of LifesPermissionSlip.com works with successful entrepreneurs who are frazzled, burned out and frustrated. He supports you to wrestle your life back from your business and give yourself permission to enjoy your success and have true prosperity.

Planned Procrastination

Procrastination seems to be a naughty word. It is blamed for our being late, missing deadlines and not doing our best. What if you could use procrastination to your advantage...and actually plan for it?

If you have tried other strategies and still find that procrastinating is the best approach to some tasks, work with your brain to make the most of the hyperfocus and energy that come naturally. For instance, forego weekly bill paying and instead plan to stay up late on one Friday night per month to get them paid and in the mail. Plan on ignoring boring daily housework, knowing that weekend visitors will have you motivated to get the house back in order, lickity-split.

Planning for procrastination means that you are purposely putting something aside with the plan of doing it later, when you can use that natural procrastination energy to focus on that task and finally get it done.

~Laurie Dupar, PMHNP, RN, PCC, Certified ADHD Coach and Nurse Practitioner

Laurie Dupar is a professional Certified Coach with over nine years of specialty in working with ADHD. Reach her at (916) 791-1799 or www.coachingforadhd.com.

Cultivate Self-Awareness: Reality Check

Take a realistic inventory of your strengths and challenges: who you are and aren't, what you are likely to do or not. Avoid sugar-coating things, but also acknowledge all you have accomplished, even if it's not quite up to your sometimes overly-critical standards of what you *should* be able to do.

Think about the things you do well, your talents and areas of competency. Be mindful of what gets you going and what shuts you down, and how this impacts your self-identity and relationships with others. There are many coaching exercises that help with this process.

Without self-awareness, you risk designing a life that may look good conceptually but doesn't work for you. When you know who you are and how you function (or not), you can develop effective strategies that work with your strengths and compensate for your challenges to create a life that fits!

~Susan Lasky, MA, BCC, SCAC

Susan Lasky, Master ADD/ADHD Strategist, Productivity Coach & Professional Organizer, creator of the 7-Step PowerPlan to Success™ and the 28-Day Accountability Challenge™. www.SusanLasky.com ~ www.PowerPlanToSuccess.com ~ Susan@SusanLasky.com

Love the Brain You're With

The ADHD brain doesn't work the same way as the typical brain, so ADDers need to find different ways to accomplish their goals. When brains fall short, an arsenal of tools and techniques can help you reach your goals. A simple kitchen timer or a smart phone app can make all the difference. The internet is full of solutions that can be tweaked and adapted for your needs.

The key is to find the right tool for your brain. Don't give up until you find something that DOES work, not something that merely SHOULD work. With that support, you can focus on what your brain does well.

The disabled runner with titanium prosthetic limbs and the elderly person with a walker have found a way to get from point A to point B, and so can you! If you can't have the brain you want, love the brain you're with.

~Mindy Schwartz Katz, MS, ACC

Mindy Schwartz Katz, ADHD/Life Coach, helps ADDers get over, around and through obstacles that get in the way of living their unique life. www.yourlife-planb.com ~ mindy@yourlife-planb.com

Focus on What You Want in Order to Feel Good and Fuel Your Vision

Quantum physics teaches that outcomes are transformed by the witness. Energy and form flow from the focus of the witness. Focusing on one's most expansive, empowering vision raises the vibrational energy to a sufficient degree to launch the dream. Standing in the future, from the point where the dream is realized, and being, seeing, doing from that specific point of view not only makes one feel great but creates the velocity to fly by any obstacles. Looking back at the present from the future allows one to coach himself regarding the efficient path with which he reached his destination. Focusing on the road blocks and the problems creates a clear path to a crash and burn and a very low vibration: a very shame-based state of feeling AWFUL. Focus, think and be what empowers and thrills you. Focus is your MAGIC WAND.

~Nancy Anne Brighton, LCSW, ADHD Coach

Nancy Anne Brighton, LCSW, ADHD Coach, empowers gifted adults with upside-down brilliance to create compelling futures from the future. Bright Brains Building. Brighter Future. www.BrightONBrains.com ~ ADHDcoach@BrightonBrains.com ~ (386) 290-6703

Dinner Preparation Without Distraction

Dinner time is a challenging time in my house: deciding what to prepare, finding the ingredients, locating the steps in the recipe...*finding* the recipe. Since I'm not the best cook, all of these pieces take tremendous thought and energy. Now imagine having to do that while caring for your two children under age four! The solution is creating distraction for young kids. Try these tips:

1. Create a marble run using empty toilet paper rolls: paint the rolls, paste magnets on them and have child arrange them on refrigerator so the marble goes through them all.

2. Post a whiteboard/chalkboard on kitchen wall for doodling, games, etc.

3. Make a glitter jar: Fill a glass jar with water, glitter and food coloring...shake and they will be mesmerized!

4. Play Easter: Right before dinner prep time, hide 10 eggs and have child find them, open them and count what they find inside. Then have them hide the eggs for you!

~Meg Gehan, LCSW

Meg Gehan, LCSW, is the owner of Outside the Box Marketing, where she helps her clients find more time to do the work they love. http://outsidetheboxmarking.org

Make the Professor Think You are Listening

Situation: Listening to professors talk just puts me to sleep! Most professors are not very entertaining and sometimes the topic is not very interesting. Whether my mind drifts or I'm falling asleep, my notes are worthless. I feel note-taking is a waste of time.

Technique: Whether your mind drifts off into la-la land or you feel yourself falling asleep (head bobbing, eyes shutting), alert yourself, look at the instructor and write down the next two or three words spoken. Don't worry about them making sense. At the end of the class, you'll have created a list of terms or topics discussed. Get out your text book or get on the internet to find out what you missed. Then the professor will gladly help answer further questions. And, he won't catch you sleeping or have to hear some lousy excuse that you're just not a good note-taker.

~Joyce Kubik, ADHD Coach, CC (IAC)

Joyce Kubik, Certified Life and ADHD Coach for students and adults, author of planning journals developed specifically for ADHD. Find it and more at www.bridgetosuccess.net.

Doodle to Boost Your Attention and Memory

Doodling or "mindless creating and shading in of shapes" can actually help your brain work better. In one study, 40 participants were monitored while they listened to a monotonous mock telephone message for the names of people coming to a party. Half of the group was randomly assigned to doodle; they shaded printed shapes while listening to the telephone call. The other group just listened. The doodling group performed better on the monitoring task and recalled 29% more information on a surprise memory test!*

So, doodle away and boost your brainpower.

*Andrade, J. (2009). "What Does Doodling Do?" Journal of Applied Cognitive Psychology, 24, 100-106.

~Roland Rotz, Ph.D. & Sarah D. Wright, M.S.

Roland Rotz, Ph.D., and Sarah D. Wright, M.S., are authors of *Fidget to Focus*, a handbook of strategies for living more easily with ADHD. www.FidgetToFocus.com

Transitions Without Meltdowns

Children with ADHD have a hard time adjusting to new situations or transitioning from one activity to another and usually don't like surprises. Give them a warning such as, "Today we are going to visit Grandma," or "In 20 minutes we need to go to bed," or "In 30 minutes we are going to the store." Prepare them, use a timer, and repeat the reminder at least a couple of times. Get their attention and respect that they are involved in another activity (probably one that they like) and don't want to be interrupted. Validate their feelings by saying, "I know you want to continue playing, however, soon it will be time to go/do something else..." Recognizing their need for transition time and preparing them for it reduces the unwanted meltdowns.

~Sherry Clarke, MA, LCMFT, ACG

Sherry Clarke, MA, LCMFT, a veteran Licensed Marriage and Family Therapist and ADHD Coach, has a passion for helping couples and parents understand, embrace and celebrate their ADHD. www.clarkecoaching.com

Cafeteria Concentration

One of the most distracting stimulus ADD people encounter is often not *external* noise, but *internal* noise. Internal noise includes extraneous ideas, tangential thoughts, and mental to-do lists. It is this internal noise that frequently distracts a person from the task at hand.

If external noise can be turned up a notch, so the theory goes, internal noise can settle down. Of course, the external noise and commotion cannot be too loud or too distracting or else the balancing act between the external and internal noise is thrown off.

The commotion at a cafeteria, coffee shop, waiting rooms or airports often have just the right amount of the noise and motion to help kinesthetic learners reduce their internal noise so they can get things done.

Where do you find it best to concentrate?

~Judith Kohlberg, Author

Judith Kolberg, author, *Conquering Chronic Disorganization* and *ADD-Friendly Ways to Organize Your Life.* www.squallpress.net

Cut to the Chase

We live in a world where technology changes overnight. Keeping up with all the upgrades, emails and texts, along with the rest of our lives, has our brains overloaded. As we all try to cope with this fast pace, our attention spans are shrinking. It's almost as if the whole world has suddenly gone ADD!

When we communicate with others, particularly in the business setting, we need to focus like a laser beam on the heart of the matter. We need to learn to "bottom line" more effectively. Getting results quickly is the expectation, and people are demanding short, concise answers, not rambling descriptions.

The bottom line: take advantage of your wonderful ADHD brain to think through issues in your own style, and then speak succinctly, listen well, and cut to the chase.

~Paul O'Connor, MCC

Paul O'Connor coaches business executives with ADHD. He is a Master Certified Coach, secretary of the Professional Association of ADHD Coaches, based in Atlanta. (404) 377-4712 paul@EnergyForLifeCoach.com ~ www.EnergyForLifeCoach.com

Up Your Grades: How to Turn Those Bs and Cs into As and Bs

Lucky you with ADHD: your natural charm and personality will go a long way to influence how your teacher grades you. To get that grade bumped up:

- Go see your teachers during their posted office hours and ask questions to ease confusions.
- Talk to other students to find out the real scoop, which teachers/professors to avoid, etc. www.ratemyprofessor.com
- Ask for copies of old exams. All they can say is no.
- Introduce yourself to your teacher/professor. Putting a face with a name will be a big help, especially if your grade is on the borderline.
- Respect is always appreciated.
- Avoid things that irritate instructors, such as:
    o Sleeping in class
    o Brown nosing
    o Not going to class
    o Lack of responsibility
    o Not reading syllabus
    o Excuses
    o Not meeting deadlines

~Anonymous

Family Meeting Magic!

For families dealing with ADHD, whether there are 10 of you or 2, meetings bring members together and build collaboration, communication and connection, all of which are vital for a happy and healthy family. For effective and fun meetings:

1. SAVE the DATE! Meet at the same time and day weekly.

2. Open with a favorite song, or share jokes or stories.

3. Use a "talking stick" or other novel object. The person holding it is the ONLY one talking.

4. Have active listeners reflect back what they heard the speaker share.

5. Use a timer to keep the meeting on track.

6. Assign positions like president, secretary, etc.

7. Laugh together!

8. Plan a game or have a special dessert afterwards.

9. Post minutes for all to see and make them understandable for younger kids.

10. Make a suggestion box and discuss entries in meetings.

~Melissa Fahrney, M.A., CPC

Melissa Fahrney, certified ADHD Coach and School Psychologist, specializes in heart-centered coaching for students and adults. "Add Heart Power to Power the Mind." www.addheartworks.com

Teach Your Child to Self-Motivate

In response to, "What do you need to do to get back on task?" teach your child to reply, "I need a motivator!" When Diane's son learned to create an incentive for himself (usually something to do with ice cream), he started finishing his homework in record speed. The ADHD brain needs motivation to maintain focus. When our kids learn this, it's liberating for everyone!

1. Educate your kids about how their ADHD shows up (e.g. "Did you notice that your brain focuses well when there is something you really want at the other end?").
2. Have them begin to create their own motivators (e.g. "What reward can you use to motivate your brain?").
3. Encourage them to pull from a tool box of tricks.

Next thing you know, they will be off and running on their own!

~ Elaine Taylor-Klaus, CPCC, ACC, and Diane Dempster, MHSA, CPC, ACC

ImpactADHD helps parents help kids. Elaine Taylor-Klaus & Diane Dempster provide reality-based training, with coaching to make it stick. We help your family thrive! http://www.ImpactADHD.com

College Freshman: I Wish Someone had Told Me...

- Go to class.
- Be on time to class.
- Ask for help.
- **College is not a contest**. Learn at your own pace.
- **Support systems are essential for survival.** Make friends. Talk to everyone.
- **Expect to feel lonely, frightened, and isolated.** Remember: You are not the only person experiencing these emotions, and it gets better.
- **Read what you are given!**
- **Join in all the activities you can.**
- **Don't be intimidated by the faculty and staff.** Your tuition dollars pay the salaries of the university.
- **Your college catalog is your Bible.** You have to open it in order to know what is inside.
- **Read a copy of your school's code of ethics**. A simple mistake could cost you your degree.
- **Maintain a positive attitude.**

~Anonymous

Couples & ADHD: Remember to Remember

Without some outside assistance, remembering to remember something in the future seems nearly impossible for people with ADHD. Outside assistance doesn't always mean turning to your partner, saying, "Remind me to do that," and then forgetting about it. That type of "memory hand off" quickly gets old and leads to resentment and failure.

Even worse is forgetting to do something that you promised your partner you would do and instead of admitting your mistake, you turn it around and blame your partner for not reminding you! Remember, a reminder from your partner is a luxury, not a right. Instead of relying on your partner, develop back-up systems like leaving yourself a voicemail, sending yourself a text message, or keeping post-its in the car and putting notes on your rear-view mirror.

~ Sarah A. Ferman, L.M.F.T., P.C.C.
& Robert L. Wilford, Ph.D.

Sarah Ferman, L.M.F.T., P.C.C., & Robert Wilford, Ph.D., are leading ADHD Couples Consultants, helping ADHD Couples reconnect and create loving and enduring relationships. www.ADHDCouplesConsultants.com

Increase Your Ap-TBI-tude!

I'm encouraging all ADDers to become aware of Traumatic Brain Injury issues and treatments. Due to hyperactivity, inattention, and high-risk activities, ADDers are at increased risk of suffering TBI in their lifetimes. According to Russell Barkley, "About one in five ADHD children is an acquired case," due to either prenatal or postnatal brain injury. If you suffer TBI, maintain a hopeful attitude and invest in cognitive rehabilitation and psychotherapy. With persistence, attitude, and treatment, you might be able to rehab better than you were before. Neurofeedback, H.I.T., SPLT, and HBOT are just a few treatments which may refine, strengthen, or create new abilities, such as information processing, memory, knowledge, language, hierarchical cognitive organization, multi-tasking, and social skills. As a result of powerful rehabilitation and persistence, my memory after my traumatic brain injury is better than before the injury. Learn what you can do to supercharge your TBI brain!

~Jonathan Salem, M.S.

Jonathan Salem, M.S. Specializes in Entrepreneurship, Applied Technology, and coaching clients with ADHD and/or Mild to Moderate Traumatic Brain Injury. (409) ADHD-NOW (409) 234-3669 ~ Jon@CoachADHDNow.com

More Protein = More Productivity

Protein helps with concentration and effective ADHD management. Here are 5 key tips to eat more protein:

1. **Chicken** – Marinade 5 chicken breasts in Italian dressing overnight, then BBQ on the grill until tender. Chop these up and put in several small plastic containers in your fridge.

2. **Eggs** – Hard-boil and peel one dozen eggs, and put 2 each in small zip lock bags.

3. **Smoothies** – Put a canister of whey protein and oatmeal on your counter. Keep frozen fruit in your freezer. Blend together ¾ cup water, ½ cup orange juice, ¾ cup frozen fruit, 1 scoop whey protein, and ¼ cup dry oatmeal for a tasty breakfast smoothie!

4. **Protein bars** – Great varieties to keep on hand are Lara and Luna Protein.

5. **Cottage cheese** – Put ½ cup cottage cheese in small plastic containers; add ¼ cup washed berries when ready to eat.

~ Elizabeth Anderson, Fitness Expert

Elizabeth Anderson, fitness expert, speaker specializing in INSIDE-OUT transformation. Go to www.elizabethanderson.com for your free "Cooking for Your Week in an Hour System."

Frustrated? Unleash That Pent-Up Energy!

I had a client who was very frustrated. He had tried, but couldn't see how to fit exercise into his busy schedule. His goal was to work out four times a week, but he was lucky to fit it in once a week. When we reframed his goal as a challenge, the competitor within him became motivated. Suddenly, all that pent-up energy had an outlet. He set a challenge to work out for 30 days straight, and he met his challenge.

His strategy worked because he was willing to try something different, and because he was able to tap into all the energy that often gets bottled-up in frustration.

Emulating his approach is something we can all do. Find an issue that you're frustrated about, and then look at new options to deal with it. Find a technique or approach that works for you, unleash that energy, and ride it to success!

~Paul O'Connor, MCC

Paul O'Connor coaches business executives with ADHD. He is a Master Certified Coach, secretary of the Professional Association of ADHD Coaches, based in Atlanta. (404) 377-4712 paul@EnergyForLifeCoach.com ~ www.EnergyForLifeCoach.com

The Planner Police

Having a planner or "reminder" system is one of the foundations of better managing your ADHD challenges. As an ADHD coach, I know how difficult it is for most people to create and actively keep a consistent planner. Not wanting to be a "planner police," I have narrowed keeping a planner down to three essential rules.

1. Have <u>one</u>. Keep all of your reminders, dates, and appointments in one place. It doesn't matter if it is electronic or paper, as long as it is all together.

2. Plan out a week in advance. Looking ahead helps you remember activities and allows you time to make adjustments to the week ahead.

3. Check in and out daily. Make a habit of looking at your planner for that day's activities and reviewing it again at day's end to see what needs to be deleted, delegated or done the next day.

~Laurie Dupar, PMHNP, RN, PCC, Certified ADHD Coach and Nurse Practitioner

Laurie Dupar lives in the greater Sacramento, CA, area and is a nationally-recognized expert on ADHD. You can reach her at (916) 791-1799 or www.coachingforadhd.com.

"As a single footstep will not make a path on the earth, so a single thought will not make a pathway in the mind.
To make a deep physical path, we walk again and again.
To make a deep mental path, we must think over and over the kind of thoughts we wish to dominate our lives."

~ Henry David Thoreau

Couples & ADHD: Staying Connected

Today, couples rely on cell phones for all kinds of communications, from sending quick "love you" texts to checking in on dinner plans. Cell phones make staying connected with your partner much easier, but keeping your cell phone charged can be challenging. Few things are more discouraging than explaining to your partner that you didn't return their call or text because your cell phone was dead. It is easy to forget to charge your phone or for "talkers" to run out of battery. Eliminate that problem by purchasing a handful of chargers, leaving one in the car, one at home, and one at the office. Finally, keep an extra wall charger in your briefcase, purse or backpack; that way you will never be caught with off guard with a dead phone. After-market chargers are inexpensive and available online at Amazon and eBay; a small investment now can save heartache later.

~ Sarah A. Ferman, L.M.F.T., P.C.C.
& Robert L. Wilford, Ph.D.

Sarah Ferman, L.M.F.T., P.C.C., & Robert Wilford, Ph.D., are leading ADHD Couples Consultants, helping ADHD Couples reconnect and create loving and enduring relationships. www.ADHDCouplesConsultants.com

"The Only Thing That Ever Sat its Way to Success was a Hen!"

One of my clients was struggling in college. He was having a hard time studying, going to classes, etc., so it wasn't easy for him to pass his classes. At the time we started our sessions, he was reading a book which said, "Whatever you dream of can come true." One day in our session, he started to cry. He said he was continuously dreaming of getting high grades, but the results were the same. My only question to him was: "What actions are taking to make your dream come true?" His answer was a long pause. Yes, our dreams can come true only if our dreams are achievable and we take action to accomplish those dreams. As Sarah Brown said, "The only thing that ever sat its way to success was a hen!"

~Pinar Kobaş, ADHD Expert

Pınar Kobas, Mental Health Counselor and ADHD Expert with ADHD. She lives in Turkey. www.dehbka.com ~ pkobas@dehbka.com

Sing Yourself into Doing Chores!

There are some simple, repetitive-type tasks where we tend to hit the Wall of Inaction. Maybe you are fine with doing the laundry but can't seem to fold the clean clothes and linens. Or you get that far, but putting away the folded laundry seems to require Herculean effort. Perhaps your hurdle is emptying the dishwasher, taking out the recycling or paying bills. You can psych yourself into action with music!

One option is to play music that claims to help your brain relax or energize, and many people find this helps. Or create your own songs. Imagine words that you associate with doing the chore. Rewrite an existing song or nursery rhyme to suit the task, "Fold, fold, fold the laundry, get it off the bed," or create a song from scratch. Have fun with this - you CAN sing yourself to success. Let me know how it goes!

~Susan Lasky, MA, BCC, SCAC

Susan Lasky, Master ADD/ADHD Strategist, Productivity Coach & Professional Organizer, creator of the 7-Step PowerPlan to Success™ and the 28-Day Accountability Challenge™. www.SusanLasky.com ~ www.PowerPlanToSuccess.com ~ Susan@SusanLasky.com

Relieve Your STRESS: Visit Your Local Watering Hole

No, we're not advocating heavy drinking to manage stress (although some certainly give it a try). Stress, caused by an automatic process, happens every time you feel threatened. The threat could be obvious, like a crisis (e.g. avoiding a car accident), or subtle, like feeling overwhelmed (e.g. a long to-do list). The threat cycle produces hormones that shut down most of your brain and bodily functions and direct your attention to your feet, so you can either fight or run away. When your animal instincts kick in, you no longer have full access to the problem-solving part of your brain. Here's a great trick: When you notice yourself feeling stressed, take a few sips of water to calm down and get back on track. It actually tricks your animal brain into thinking, "We've stopped at a watering hole; the threat must have passed." Crazy, but it really works!

~Elaine Taylor-Klaus, CPCC, ACC & Diane Dempster, MHSA, CPC, ACC

ImpactADHD helps parents help kids. Elaine Taylor-Klaus & Diane Dempster provide reality-based training, with coaching to make it stick. We help your family thrive! http://www.ImpactADHD.com

Everything Needs a Home

When I talk with clients about The Family Coach Method concept of living in damage control, I often hear "What's the one thing I can do today to get out of damage control?" The answer: "Give all your important personal items *one home*." One of the greatest challenges in ADHD is inattention. An aspect of inattention is behaving automatically instead of intentionally. The way to help yourself manage automaticity is to put all your important items in one place - the same place - every single moment of every day. Your keys, wallet, phone, birth certificates, eye glasses, passport, briefcase, backpack, favorite shoes, and so on: one place for each item.

Go now! Get up and look around your home and choose *the home* for each valued item. When you develop the discipline to "live your systems" and make a home for everything, life will be easier.

~*Lynne Kenney, Psy.D.*

Lynne Kenney, Psy.D., is a mother of two, a practicing pediatric psychologist in Scottsdale, AZ, and the creator of The Family Coach Method. Her NEW co-authored book, *Time-In not Time-Out*, is available this Fall on Kindle. For more visit www.lynnekenney.com.

Swiss Cheese Report Cards

It used to be we thought if you had ADHD, you were not smart and if you are smart, you can't have ADHD. In fact, most people with ADHD have above-normal intelligence. However, being smart doesn't mean that your child can't get below-average grades or that short-term memory challenges or distractibility, common ADHD symptoms, can't play a role.

How to know if your child is challenged with short-term memory? They often have "Swiss cheese" report cards. Interestingly, bright students will get A's or B's on in-class exams/quizzes but have glaring holes or 0's in homework categories because they can't remember to complete - or turn in - their homework.

If this is your child, take heart; they are capable and just need some planning and organizing strategies to fill those homework gaps. The problem is not intelligence or responsibility, it is distractibility and remembering!

~Laurie Dupar, PMHNP, RN, PCC, Certified ADHD Coach and Nurse Practitioner

Laurie Dupar is an internationally-recognized ADHD expert, trained psychiatric mental health nurse practitioner and certified ADHD Coach. Contact her at www.coachingforadhd.com or (916) 791-1799.

The IN/OUT Ratio

Ever wonder how much needs to go out or how much you can keep in order to get yourself organized? Judith Kolberg, author of *Conquering Chronic Disorganization*, offers this tip for how to balance what to discard and what to keep in order to reach your goal:

1:1   One old item out for every new item in will control your collection at its current level.

1:2   Two old items out for every new item in will slowly diminish your old collection as you upgrade with new items.

1:3   Three old items out for every one item in will begin to replace your old collection with new items **and** decrease your overall collection.

1:5   Five old items out for every new item in will decrease your overall collection *permanently* and leave you with only the very best of your existing collection.

~Judith Kolberg, Author

Judith Kolberg, author, *Conquering Chronic Disorganization* and *ADD-Friendly Ways to Organize Your Life*. www.squallpress.net

Looking Left and Right

I see it in business all the time: Looking left and right to see what everyone else is doing. And why are we looking left and right? Competition. But no other business can be like yours. YOU are what makes your service, product, or program uniquely yours. Here are a few pointers to keep you from judging and comparing yourself, so that the BEST you is always present:

1. Hold your hand up in front of you. Look at your fingertips. No one else has those. Only you. Remember, there is no competition or comparison. Look straight ahead.

2. Feeling behind? Stop and take stock. You're only behind if you are doing it someone else's way. Look straight ahead.

3. Be grateful. You simply cannot feel competitive, angry, or envious if you are in a state of gratefulness. Look straight ahead.

Stay on purpose- look ahead and keep changing the world!

~Suzanne Evans, CEO

Suzanne Evans is the founder of Suzanne Evans Coaching, LLC, ranked #225 in Inc 500 for 2012. She supports, coaches, and teaches over 30,000 women enrolled in her wealth and business-building programs.

Taming the Chaos

Whether we have ADHD or not, there seem to be specific areas that consistently keep our lives from turning into unmanageable chaos. These are: taking the time to plan, having a paper management system and writing things down.

1. Having time to organize is important. I set aside 30 minutes at the start of my day to review my schedule and look at what my priorities are for the day.

2. For managing paperwork, I have a small file drawer near my desk. Most often this "drawer" is open so I can easily see its contents with quick access to frequently-used documents.

3. Finally, a must is to write everything down! Even though I am a fairly organized person with most of my memory still intact, if it's not written down it never existed!

~Laurie Dupar, PMHNP, RN, PCC,
Certified ADHD Coach

Laurie Dupar, Certified ADHD Coach, is a internationally-recognized ADHD expert and author of the book, *Brain Surfing & 31 other Awesome Qualities of ADHD*. www.coachingforadhd.com

Get in the Mood with Visualization & Go Step by Step!

Packing can be a big issue for an ADHDer. My secret is to visualize the day in my mind. I include all the details: waking up, taking a shower, washing my face, brushing my teeth, etc., and finally getting dressed. I think about all of the materials I need to do all of these steps. If I take pills, which ones? Where will I go on that trip? Is it to the school, to the beach, skiing? What kind of materials do I need to go to the beach (swimsuits, towels, sunscreen, etc.)? Then I visualize the rest of the day, thinking of each day of the trip so that if one day I will do something different, I will remember to bring the necessary items. Then I ask, what else? A book, my passport? Finally, what do I want to find ready when I come back? Just visualize and ask questions out loud; the answers will come.

~Suzan Tana Alalu, MA, ACC, PACG

Suzan Tana Alalu, MA in Psychology and Expressive Arts, ACC, Professional ADHD Coach in Turkey, specializes in transforming your attention and relationship systems. talalu@dehbka.com

Advice to a Parent...From a Former Kid

The most important thing you can do for your kids is, above all else, to love them. Help them see that they are lovable, no matter what challenges or mistakes they make. Making mistakes is necessary to learn and grow. No one is perfect. Let them know that they don't have to be perfect to be lovable and worthy people. Help your kids find their strengths: the things they are good at. The world is, and will always be, full of people who are ready to point out their weaknesses and failures. Most people with ADHD or other learning problems hear about their weaknesses so much that they take on that role as who they are. Help your kid to find his/her strengths because ultimately, that is where they will find success in life. That is truly a gift.

~Rose Smith, M. Ed.

Rose Smith, M. Ed. For more helpful hints and random reflections, please visit http://RandomReflectionsbyRose.wordpress.com/.

ADHD: Social Learning Disability, or Both?

Individuals diagnosed with ADHD usually have difficulty with social skills, even though they may be extremely "sociable." However, some children diagnosed with ADHD are extremely challenged socially; their parents and teachers often describe them as children who "just don't get it." These children usually have no idea why they are being punished and why they are told that they are inappropriate at times. Rigidity and a high degree of naivety usually accompany Social Learning Disorder (SLD), which makes dealing with it very difficult.

Social Learning Disorder usually affects the learning process as well, as these children could easily misinterpret the idea behind a book and/or an argument. I highly suggest that, when in doubt, the parents contact a professional who could rule out this disability or, if it exists, to treat it accordingly.

~Roya Kravetz, ACC, BCC, CMC

Roya Kravetz, Credentialed and Board-Certified Life Coach, Certified Executive Coach, Instructor and Speaker specializing in ADHD Family & Relationship Coaching. www.adhdsuccesscoaching.com ~ (858) 334-8584

General Tips for the Elder ADDer

ADD symptoms worsen when you stop working and have NO structure. So create structure . . . make a schedule of activities and stick to it, just like you did when you had to. If you don't have any regular activities, get some! Volunteer. Write a book. Take up painting or knitting. Walk dogs. Grow vegetables. Play bridge or bingo. Take an exercise class. Help others. Keep busy; stay engaged in life.

Time on our hands makes us ADDers run in circles and get into trouble. Following a schedule keeps us balanced. If you have lived for decades with ADD, you will have unknowingly developed strategies for dealing with it; keep using them in your new schedule, and don't let anyone tell you you're wrong. If it works for you, it's right!

Don't keep your ADD a secret; people need to know that we elders have ADD, too.

~Jane Patrick, BA, MEd.

Jane Patrick, retired teacher, diagnosed with ADD at age 75. Now enjoying the trip! Advocate for neglected group of 60+ ADDers. janeham@abacocm.com

So Many Choices...

Managing your ADHD is an ongoing process. Below are some of my top picks of helpful, accurate resources.

Conferences/events/symposiums to attend in person:

- Children and Adults with Attention Deficit Disorder, www.CHADD.org (International)
- Attention Deficit Disorder Association, www.ADD.org (International)
- ADD Resources, www.ADDresources.org (Seattle, WA)
- ADHD Aware, www.ADHDAware.org (Pennsylvania)

Telesummits (virtual conferences you can attend by phone):

- Succeed with ADHD Telesummit: Host, Laurie Dupar, www.succeedwithadhdtelesummit.com
- Virtual ADHD conference: Host, Jennifer Koretsky, www.virtualADHDConference.com
- ADHD Awareness Expo: Host, Tara McGillicuddy, http://www.adhdexpo.com/

Radio talk shows:

- ADHD Support Talk Radio: Host, Tara McGillicuddy, http://www.blogtalkradio.com/add-adhd-coaching
- Attention Talk Radio: Host, Jeff Copper, http://www.blogtalkradio.com/attentiontalkradio

~ Laurie Dupar, ADHD Coach & Expert

Laurie Dupar is an internationally-recognized ADHD expert, author and ADHD Coach. You can reach her at www.coachingforadhd.com or (916) 791-1799.

Choosing to Sail

Have you experienced what it's like to study when you're fresh and alert? How is that different from when you're tired, hungry, and restless? It's probably like the difference between sailing a catamaran on a beautiful, breezy day and rowing against the current in a gale. Which would you rather do?

In your daily life, you can make those same choices.

Identify when you tend to be focused and alert: is it in the morning, in the evening, after exercising? Then plan, or better yet *schedule*, time in your agenda to do the demanding work when you're in that optimal state of mind. Save the busy work, errands, and exercise for when you're restless and less focused.

~Sarah D. Wright, M.S., A.C.T.

Nationally-known ADHD coach Sarah D. Wright specializes in helping professionals in small businesses get on track and get going. FocusForEffectiveness.com ~ Sarah@FocusForEffectiveness.com (858) 408-9338.

Act, Don't Think! Wait, What?

Today, I challenge you to tackle that task *without thinking about it first*! Just walk into that dirty, cluttered garage with a plastic bag and just start putting stuff inside! Don't stop and stand at that garage door thinking about having to organize all that junk or about how long it's going to take to clean the garage, or it won't get done! Just start stuffing. When the bag is full, get another bag and do it again! What you'll find is that at some point during the process, you will start thinking to yourself about what you want to tackle next, and when that happens, just keep going because then you are safe. You are into the task and it has become interesting! Before you know it, you will be done and will have a tool to try again!

~Sandy Alletto Corbin, MA, ACG, SCAC

Sandy Alletto Corbin, a Senior Credentialed ADHD Coach and teacher, woman with ADHD and a single mother of an ADHD daughter, specializes in coaching women, teens and college students and advocating for change. www.lifecoachsandyalletto.com

ADHD, Asperger's and Eye Contact

Many people with both Asperger's Syndrome and ADHD have difficulty making eye contact. Just because they are not looking at you does not mean that they aren't paying attention. In fact, they may be paying greater attention to what you are saying than if they were looking at you. Making eye contact can be very distracting for them, causing them to not completely process what you are saying. So before you judge them and think they are not listening to you because they aren't looking at you, wait for their response and you may find a more complete answer than you would have gotten had they made eye contact.

~Dana D. Maher, Life Coach

Dana D. Maher, Personal and Executive Life Coach for adolescents and adults, including those with Asperger's Syndrome and ADHD. ddmaher@yahoo.com ~ 908-377-8427

Level the Playing Field

It's helpful to understand the process when your teen is in high school facing the often dreaded ACT or College Board exams. Although your teen may have accommodations on a 504 plan or IEP, s/he will not automatically get the same accommodations on ACT or College Board exams (including PSAT, SAT and AP tests). Because the process can take at least several months, you need to start as early as possible. The tests are not "flagged," so prospective colleges and universities will not know that students took the tests with accommodations. Your teen's guidance counselor should be able to help you. You might also go to www.ACTstudent.org or http://student.collegeboard.org and follow the links for students with disabilities. Don't hesitate to request accommodations, if needed. In doing so, you are "leveling the playing field" so the test results will adequately reflect your teen's knowledge and skills. For more tips, visit www.FocusForEffectiveness.com/blog.

~Roxanne Fouche, ADHD Coach

Roxanne Fouche, ADHD Coach, helps both students and women live successfully with ADHD and related challenges. In person, phone, or Skype. Contact (858) 484-4749 or Roxanne@FocusForEffectiveness.com.

Thinking Outside the "Box"

Having a hard time motivating yourself to do something unpleasant? Get creative!

Recently, I had been putting off cleaning the cat box. I could not find it within myself to begin the task. I really, really, really did not want to do this unexciting and unpleasant task! Then I remembered a method I used to use to motivate students with multiple disabilities to do things they weren't happy about or were having difficulty starting; I'd make up a song about it! It worked. I sang about how bad it was as I cleaned out the litter and it became almost fun - certainly bearable. If you are finding it hard to do things like doing the dishes, yard work or other mundane or unpleasant tasks, try singing yourself through it. It worked for me!

~Aimee Green, MLIS, MSSW, ADHD Coach

Aimee Green MLIS, MSSW, ADHD Coach & Organizer for Adults & College Students. Austin, Texas www.austinADDcoaching.com ~ aimee@aimeegreen.net ~ (512) 230-5477

Best Seat in the House

Where we sit in a classroom, office or even at the dinner table can have a lot to do with how well we can pay attention and get things done. If we are seated too close to a door, the activity could be enough to get us off track. If we sit facing a window, movement from outside can distract us from the task at hand. If we are seated next to someone who's restless, their fidgetiness can be enough to drive us crazy.

Having the best seat in the house may not mean up front, next to a teacher or boss, or by the person who "always gets the job done." The best seat is the one that for YOU has the fewest distractions or, alternatively, enough distractions to keep you interested.

The best seat is the one that helps YOU focus, get the job done and feel successful.

~Laurie Dupar, PMHNP, RN, PCC Certified ADHD Coach and Nurse Practitioner

Laurie is a trained mental health nurse practitioner and professional certified coach specializing in people with ADHD. You can reach her online at www.coachingforadhd.com or by phone at (916) 791-1799.

"The road to success is not straight. There is a curve called a failure. A loop called confusion. Speed bumps called friends. Caution lights called family. "You will have flat tires called jobs. But if you have a spare called determination. An engine called perseverance. A driver called God, you will make it to a place called success."

~ Anonymous

Author Index

Get your complimentary BONUS Audio CD and co-author extras at:

http://theadhdawarenessbookproject.com/3651-order-page

Have the audio CD shipped to your doorstep and get access to additional co-author interviews and bonuses such as:

- A sneak peak of Dr. Billi's upcoming book and learn how to Leverage ADHD to your ADDvantage

- Paul O'Conner's report on success strategies for ADHD business owners

- Susan Lasky's, The 7-Step to Success™ with ADHD pdf handout, and

- Interviews and more ADHD success strategies with Abigail Wurf, Sarah Wright, Sarah Ferman, Dr. Robert L. Wilford, Elaine Taylor-Klaus and Diane Dempster

Register your Amazon receipt and mailing information and we will ship you your BONUS CD complete with 8 exceptional ADHD experts sharing more great tips and resources, along with several other bonuses that our co-authors have provided especially to go with the book!

*Your Amazon receipt number is 17 digits long and spaced like this: 123-1234567-1234567. Just go to the URL page;

http://theadhdawarenessbookproject.com/3651-order-page

Enter your name, address and your Amazon order number: to get your BONUS CD sent out right away!

CPSIA information can be obtained at www.ICGtesting.com
Printed in the USA
BVOW011302310313

316922BV00014B/477/P